Prophesy to the Land

Prophesy to the Land

Les Lawrence

© Copyright 1994 — Les Lawrence

All rights reserved. This book is protected under the copyright laws of the United States of America. This book may not be copied or reprinted for commercial gain or profit. The use of short quotations or occasional page copying for personal or group study is permitted and encouraged. Permission will be granted upon request. Unless otherwise identified, Scripture quotations are from the New King James Version of the Bible. All emphases within the Scripture quotes are the author's own.

Take note that the name satan and related names are not capitalized. We choose not to acknowledge him, even to the point of violating grammatical rules.

Treasure House
An Imprint of
Destiny Image
P.O. Box 310
Shippensburg, PA 17257

"For where your treasure is there will your heart be also." Matthew 6:21

ISBN 1-56043-802-9

For Worldwide Distribution
Printed in the U.S.A.

Treasure House books are available through these fine distributors outside the United States:

Christian Growth, Inc. Jalan Kilang-Timor, Singapore 0315	Successful Christian Living Capetown, Rep. of South Africa
Lifestream Nottingham, England	Vision Resources Ponsonby, Auckland, New Zealand
Rhema Ministries Trading Randburg, South Africa	WA Buchanan Company Geebung, Queensland, Australia
Salvation Book Centre Petaling, Jaya, Malaysia	Word Alive Niverville, Manitoba, Canada

Inside the U.S., call toll free to order:
1-800-722-6774

Dedication

This book is dedicated to the inspiration of Pastor Earl Waterman of Dalton Mountain, New Hampshire, who said to me, "Prophesy, young man, prophesy!"

About the Cover

The cover photo is a beautiful view of the Valley of Jezreel in Israel. My wife, Doreen, took this picture on our 1988 trip to the Promised Land. In the distant background is Nazareth, Jesus' hometown. Isn't it interesting to think that Jesus spent His childhood overlooking the spot where the final battle of the ages, Armageddon, will be fought?

Acknowledgments

Great thanks go to the congregation at Maranatha Chapel for allowing me the liberty to work on this book for many hours over the past ten years, as well as for their prayers and faithful financial support. I especially want to thank my brother, Ken Lawrence, for his love and oversight through many years. I also thank my dear friends: Tim and Pam Raymond, Jerry and Mary Hurst, Steve and Kathleen Peck, Brian and Joanne Lee, Bob and Joan Ghiotto, Jeff and Sherry Ghiotto, Harold and Joann Kent, and Haim and Rachel Levi for their encouragement and understanding of my "Israel vision."

Thanks to Nancy Justice, my good friend at *Charisma* magazine for her major editorial assistance. Also, thanks to Tony Morgan for his computer expertise, which was given with the sacrifice of a true friend.

I'm also very grateful to those many friends who have believed in the value of this message and who have helped in specific tangible support of this book project. But most of all, I am very grateful for the grace of the Lord Jesus in completing this work, and to my wife Doreen, who has been my greatest help.

Contents

Foreword xiii
Preface xv

**Part I The Premise: The Faithfulness
of God's Character** 1
           Red Sea Sunrise: An Introduction 3
Chapter 1   Speak to the Dirt 9
Chapter 2   I Will Multiply Men 17
Chapter 3   No Plan B 25
Chapter 4   Is the Church Becoming
                Anti-Semitic Again? 33

**Part II The Promise: The Faithfulness
of God's Word** 41
Chapter 5   Nuts and Bolts 43
Chapter 6   Prophesy to the Bones 53
Chapter 7   World History Time Line 61
Chapter 8   The Fall and Rising of Israel 69

Chapter 9	The Contemporary Jewish Problem	77
Chapter 10	The Paradox of Jewish Salavation	85
Chapter 11	God's Faithful Covenant	93

Part III The Precision: The Faithfulness of God's Fulfillment 103

Chapter 12	Homogenous History	105
Chapter 13	The Baal Gods and Islam	113
Chapter 14	Seeing Double Double	131
Chapter 15	Tears	141
Chapter 16	Christ Killers!	153
Chapter 17	I Will Kibbutz You	165
Chapter 18	Israel at the End of the Twentieth Century	177
Chapter 19	The Wilderness on the Way to Promise	189
Chapter 20	The Church at the End of the Twentieth Century	197
	Epilogue: A Call to Action	211
	References	215

Foreword

It is an honor and a privilege to write an introduction to this very important book, which endeavors to show the Church the faithfulness of God in His promises to Israel.

I remember meeting Pastor Les Lawrence barely three years after starting Beth Israel Messianic Synagogue. Before meeting him, Messianic Jews in Tampa Bay were all alone. Some pastors were sending people to our meetings with instructions to disband us! Others used their pulpits to attack us by preaching that "Messianic Judaism is not of God" and "Jews should be in the church where they belong." I remember asking a former pastor friend of mine, who had been preaching against us on Sunday nights, if he found fault with Latinos having their own churches, or Koreans, etc. When he answered negatively, I asked him why he preached against us. He answered, "That's just it—because you are Jews! And Jews cannot have their own congregations." Isn't this the pride that Paul warned against in Romans 11:25?

God is a covenant-keeping God. His oaths never change. His plan will be fulfilled with us, the Jews; with our land; and with the true remnant of the Church, the true Christians. He has always had His people, now and in every age. His special people have joined themselves to Israel, as did Ruth the Moabitess. These are people who have been willing to die with us! They know His Word, and are not swayed by man-made theologies. They know the Word of God and His eternal promises.

At a time when we needed someone, Pastor Les Lawrence and his wife, Doreen, gave us love and encouragement. Since then, a handful of pastors in the U.S.A. have done the same.

May their names be inscribed in God's "Book of Remembrance" forever! We, the Levites, say to you: "Adonai baruch atah; the Lord bless you."

—W. Haim Levi, Messianic Jewish Rabbi,
Tampa, Florida
August, 1993—Elul 5753

(Author's Note: Rabbi Haim Levi is president of the Messianic Jewish Alliance of America, the world's largest Messianic Jewish ministry.)

Preface

This book was written to fill a gap in the perceptions of Jews and Christians alike. It is a true saying that God will accomplish His eternal purposes, either with us or without us. Nowhere is this more evident than in the issue of modern Israel. The controversy surrounding the Middle East will not diminish, however; it is destined to expand.

There is no attempt here to defend every action of Israel's present government. The focus is the prophetic purpose of the God of Abraham, Isaac, and Jacob first to the land, then to its people, and finally to all the nations of the world. In the end, God's will is done. It is this author's hope that we will not be ignorant of clear scriptural evidence unveiling the immutable purpose of God.

Part I

The Premise: The Faithfulness of God's Character

Red Sea Sunrise

An Introduction

Turquoise water...tan sand...and a tangerine sun! It was without question one of the most beautiful and indescribable sights of my 45 years. Words fail to adequately portray the splendor on that exquisite shore of the timeless Red Sea. My friend, Duane Trochessett, and I had just come from Jerusalem in January 1990. We had participated in the most powerful prayer conference we had ever attended. After speaking to a congregation in Tiberias on Shabbat, Israel's Sabbath, we traversed Israel from Galilee in the north, to the southernmost Israeli seaport of Elat. This modern city is located at the northern tip of the Red Sea. From there, we endured a rickety Egyptian public bus ride for five hours as we went further south through the Sinai Peninsula to a spot near its southernmost point. We lugged a two-man tent with us, which we pitched on a deserted stretch of Red Sea beach, a few miles north of Sharm el Sheikh, Egypt.

Prophesy to the Land

We had heard that the Red Sea had some of the most beautiful coral reefs in the world along these shores, and we were not disappointed. We walked up the pristine beach for two or three miles, seeing no one else and feeling alone in the world. We then drifted and snorkeled, swimming with the current back to our tent location among picturesque rocks on the tan beach. That the Red Sea had such underwater beauty had never occurred to me before. The Bible does not really refer to the Sea, except when mentioning how Pharaoh's chariots and army ended up there.

Our greatest sight occurred the next morning at first light. The setting was already surreal; we were in an exotic location at a time of personal renewal with God. We opened the flap on our eastward-facing tent and were stunned with the view. Rising out of the turquoise sea was the largest sun we had ever seen, almost close enough to touch. It was the most incredible shade of color; the closest I can describe it is tangerine! It was perfectly round as it rose on the horizon, resurrecting out of the water. The lack of pollution in the cloudless blue sky eliminated the sun's rays, making the stark contrast more amazing between that brilliant reddish-orange sun, the blue sky, and the turquoise sea. The only slight comparison I can make is to the occasional beautiful orange harvest moon I have seen a few times in New England. But this was the sun—a thousand times deeper in that surreal tangerine color, and a million times more radiant! Duane and I worshiped the Creator on that beach in a depth of personal connection with Him unlike any previous experience. We were not worshiping the creation, but the One who had created. As you read this book, please try to rise above the history and logic of the words to see the God of the Bible who is the Faithful God of history.

Red Sea Sunrise: An Introduction

Modern Israel has risen out of the sea of nations like that tangerine sun. In my opinion, this may be the most important book written on the subject of Israel and the Middle East in this decade because of the critical message it contains for Christians. The amazing reappearance of Israel as a nation has profound importance regarding the nature of God. He directly links His covenant with Israel to His faithful nature, as seen in all creation:

Thus says the Lord, who gives the sun for a light by day, the ordinances of the moon and the stars for a light by night, who disturbs the sea, And its waves roar (the Lord of hosts is His name): "If those ordinances depart from before Me, says the Lord, then the seed of Israel shall also cease from being a nation before Me forever" (Jeremiah 31:35-36).

Although I claim no unusual credentials as a theologian in the academic tradition, nevertheless, the proper category for this book is certainly theology. But the style I have chosen in which to present my thesis is admittedly intended for a more popular and widespread readership. I will leave the subsequent debate over the finer points to others.

However, the theological issue is clear. The nature of God's faithfulness, as a theological tenet, is being seriously undermined by Western Christian "pop theology" that divorces Christianity from its Jewish roots. But even more seriously, it *divorces God from His own character.* If God lied or changed His mind about His unconditional promises to Israel, then there would be no basis left to believe His covenant to Christians. God is either a covenant keeper or a covenant breaker. It cannot be both ways.

Hear the word of the Lord, O nations, and declare it in the isles afar off, and say, "He who scattered Israel will gather him, and keep him as a shepherd does his flock." (Jeremiah 31:10).

You shall no longer be termed Forsaken, nor shall your land any more be termed Desolate; but you shall be called Hephzibah, and your land Beulah; for the Lord delights in you, and your land shall be married. (Isaiah 62:4).

The overriding theme of this book is the faithfulness of God. The Creator has revealed Himself in many ways. He is the only true God and can be seen in all He has created (as I have testified of the glorious Red Sea sunrise). He is also revealed in the objective form of the written Word—the Holy Scriptures. Among all the ways of revelation, however, there remains a particularly clear unveiling of the faithful God in His relationship with one land and one specific people: Israel.

Of course, this is not to deny His loving relationship with all peoples who will seek Him; but it does make a profound point. All of God's activities in the entire earth are *derived* from the critical fact of His own character: *faithfulness*! Thus, how God views *eretz Israel* ("the land") over the course of history, shows the standard of integrity issuing directly from His own character. This is of utmost importance, first to the people of Israel, and then to all the other nations destined to be included in His family. The addition of the nations is foreseen, and provision for their inclusion is part of God's original plan. The biblical analogy is of one plant with branches broken off, wild branches grafted into the original plant, and finally some of the broken off branches being grafted back into the *same* planting (see Rom. 11).

Red Sea Sunrise: An Introduction

Even the Scripture record itself, with the great promise of salvation through the Messiah Yeshua (Jesus) and all the other Bible promises, *does not stand alone!* The veracity or truthfulness of the written Word is only as sure as the truthful character of the Author. The source of the Bible is the Person of God, who revealed Himself through the awesome process of many writers over many centuries of time. But if God lies or breaks His word in any way, then the *basis of believing* is lost. The word of a liar is worthless. But God speaks only truth because *God is truth!*

I believe that we are living in the last days and are in the beginning of a revival that may prove to be the greatest revival in history. God Himself is visiting all His people once again to finish what He started. So much is at stake in everything we do now that we must reconfirm our faith in the righteous character of God. We are experiencing a new boldness and fear of the Lord as God reveals His holiness and His glory.

The title of this book is taken from the command God gave to Ezekiel to prophesy to the land, or "speak to the dirt," as I have paraphrased. Ezekiel 36 may seem a strange place to start a story, but it is the basis of the whole issue I intend to clarify in this book. God's *power* is manifested in creation, but His *faithful nature* is particularly confirmed in Israel. Through an analysis of Ezekiel 36, the first three chapters of *Prophesy to the Land* lay a foundation for our study of God's character. As surely as that tangerine sun rose over the Red Sea, God is raising up Israel out of the sea of nations in prophetic fulfillment of His eternal purpose.

GOD IS FAITHFUL!

Chapter 1

Speak to the Dirt

Before we can discuss the people of promise, we must start with the covenant land. God called Ezekiel to prophesy the word of the Lord. Now, I take the Scriptures literally wherever possible, but this account in the Book of Ezekiel seems a bit odd at first glance. God sent Ezekiel around the land talking to inanimate objects. It is bad enough when you talk to yourself, but here is a man speaking to dirt. It was not easy being a prophet of God. Ezekiel was commissioned to go around Israel delivering his message to mountains, rivers, valleys, cliffs, trees, rocks and even cities; but not (at first) to people. This has to be one of the more interesting assignments ever for a prophet of God.

Ezekiel 36:1 confirms my point: "And you, son of man, prophesy to the mountains of Israel, and say, 'O mountains of Israel, hear the word of the Lord!' " In verse 4 it continues: "Therefore, O mountains of Israel, hear the word of the Lord God! Thus says the Lord God to the mountains, the hills, the rivers, the valleys, the desolate wastes, and the cities that have been forsaken, which became plunder and mockery to the rest of the nations all around." Finally it says in verse 6: "Therefore prophesy concerning the *land* of Israel, and say to the mountains, the hills, the rivers, and the valleys...." We are interested in exactly what this prophecy says, but first, just pause and absorb the fact that the prophecy is directed not to people, but to the "dirt," or the land itself! It is necessary to emphasize this point so we can understand that the promise is not simply to an ethnic people, but to an actual geographical location on the globe.

There are three reasons for why this fact is significant. First, the geographical orientation of the promise indicates that we should not lean to a symbolic or spiritualized interpretation of the prophecy. Second, it is evidence that God's promises to the people of Israel do not stand alone, but are directly connected to previously established promises to the land. The third and most important reason is what this promise says about the character of God. He is the God who *keeps* His word.

Earlier in the Book of Ezekiel the same point is stated clearly: " 'For *on* My holy mountain, on the mountain *height* of Israel,' says the Lord God, '*there* all the house of Israel, all of them in the land, shall serve Me; *there* I will accept them...' " (Ezek. 20:40). The words I have emphasized are geographical words. They refer to the land. God has made certain promises to the land that must be kept, not for the peoples' sakes, but for the integrity of the One who said it.

Isaiah 62:4 uses even stronger language: "You shall no longer be termed Forsaken, nor shall your *land* any more be termed Desolate; but you shall be called Hephzibah, *and your land Beulah*; for the Lord delights in you, *and your land shall be married."* *Beulah* is the Hebrew word for *married*. God is revealing that His commitment to the land is a marriage covenant. He would not lightly use such an analogy. God is married to the land of Israel as a specific geographic entity in the earth.

The Nature of God

God's covenant nature is on the line. "Therefore know that the Lord your God, He is God, the faithful God who keeps covenant and mercy for a thousand generations with those who love Him and keep His commandments" (Deut. 7:9). This is a monumental declaration of the nature of God. It is what theologians call an immutable fact. It cannot be canceled out, debated, or contradicted. God faithfully *keeps* His word. Now there are those who believe that the second half of the verse is a loophole allowing God to break His word if the people of some future generation stop loving Him and break His commandments. This is where you must think very carefully. You dare not misunderstand this point. An individual person or even a group may be lost through unbelief, but the original promise to Abraham and the fathers *must be kept* regardless of individuals who choose to reject God's grace. God will continue to have mercy on the descendants of Abraham, Isaac, and Jacob because He said He would! Of course the promise we have been considering in this chapter concerns the *land* of Israel. We will get to the people of Israel later.

The Oath of God

There is one more aspect of this subject we will consider before we go on to specifics about the people. No less than three references are made in Ezekiel and Isaiah to God's raising His hand in an oath. Let us consider each one in context.

I have set watchmen on your walls, O Jerusalem; they shall never hold their peace day or night. You who make mention of the Lord, do not keep silent, and give Him no rest till He establishes and till He makes Jerusalem a praise in the earth. The Lord has sworn by His right hand and by the arm of His strength: "Surely I will no longer give your grain as food for your enemies; and the sons of the foreigner shall not drink your new wine, for which you have labored. But those who have gathered it shall eat it, and praise the Lord; those who have brought it together shall drink it in My holy courts" (Isaiah 62:6-9).

This promise includes the people, but it clearly speaks of the physical land, the produce of the land of Israel as well as the specific city of Jerusalem.

The second reference to God's lifting His hand in an oath is found in Ezekiel 20:42:

*Then you shall know that I am the Lord, when I bring you into the **land** of Israel, into the **country** for which I raised My hand in an oath to give to your fathers.*

We will cover Ezekiel 20 in more detail later when we consider the peculiar phenomena that all the Jews who are leaving the nations to which they have been scattered do not automatically return directly to Israel. Nevertheless, we see another reference to God raising His Hand in an oath. Again there is a mention of the land, but this time He adds the word *country* so there can be no mistake about His promise being geographical.

The third example of this remarkable phrase is found in the chapter that is the cornerstone of this book.

Therefore thus says the Lord God: "I have raised My hand in an oath that surely the nations that are around you shall bear their own shame. But you, O mountains of Israel, you shall shoot forth your branches, and yield your fruit to My people Israel, for they are about to come" (Ezekiel 36:7-8).

Remember that the first seven verses of this passage have not been about the people at all, but about the land. God is speaking to the physical land, the literal geographical place. When He uses the personal pronoun "you" in verse 7, He is still referring to the land. Even in verse 8, where He first refers to the people, the word is addressed to the land. His oath is clearly to the land.

God's swearing by an oath and uplifted hand has to be one of the most profound studies in the Bible. Just picture it. The Holy Almighty God deems that this promise is so important that He swears to it! The idea of God's swearing an oath was such a curiosity to me that I consulted *Strong's Concordance* and was amazed to discover no less than 55 Bible verses that refer to God swearing to keep His word to the land and people of Israel! No other oath was systematically remembered even close to 55 times. Remember this New Testament passage:

For when God made a promise to Abraham, because He could swear by no one greater, He swore by Himself, saying, "Surely blessing I will bless you, and multiplying I will multiply you." And so, after he had patiently endured, he obtained the promise. For men indeed swear by the greater, and an oath for confirmation is for them an end of all dispute. Thus God, determining to show more abundantly to the heirs of promise the immutability of His counsel, confirmed it by an oath, that

> *by two immutable things, in which it is impossible for God to lie, we might have strong consolation, who have fled for refuge to lay hold of the hope set before us* (Hebrews 6:13-18).

The two unchangeable (immutable) things are the original promise itself, and then the oath sworn by God to confirm His promise. These are both resting on the unchangeable fact that it is impossible for God to lie!

The Immutability of God

I would like to define the word *immutable* for you in such a way that you will never forget. In fact, you will remember it from now on, every time you pick up your television remote control. The word *immutable* used to be a difficult concept for me to understand. The light came on for me when I thought of it in modern usage. Let's face it; nobody uses the word "immutable" in daily conversation. Then I remembered my TV remote control. What is your favorite button on your remote control? Whenever I preach this message, I ask the congregation to respond. Some simply like the "On/Off" button. Others like the channel changers; but most people agree with me. My favorite remote control button is the "Mute" button. It is so convenient. It seems to give me a sort of power—yes, even *control* over the television! If I don't like listening to a commercial, I just push the "Mute" button and I don't have to listen. Don't you agree? Even if you prefer the "On/Off" button or the channel changer button, you can see my point. There is a definite sense of control over what you see and hear.

Our problem, however, is that we live our lives as though God were a great cosmic broadcast that we could tune in/tune out, turn on/turn off; change, or mute at our own whim with our trusty little remote control devices. Many people don't like what God says or does. We don't want to listen to His voice, so we try everything we know to mute Him; but sooner or later we learn. *You can't mute God—He is immutable!* We try to make Him fit into a box. We try to change the message to something more to our liking, but it is impossible. He is unchangeable. He is in control. James 1:17 says of Him, "…with whom there is no variation or shadow of turning." Malachi 3:6 quotes the Lord: "For I am the Lord, I do not change…" and that great verse in Hebrews 13:8 says, "Jesus Christ is the same yesterday, today, and forever." *God is immutable!*

The apostle Paul spoke this principle in another context.

Therefore, when I was planning this, did I do it lightly? Or the things I plan, do I plan according to the flesh, that with me there should be Yes, Yes, and No, No? But as God is faithful, our word to you was not Yes and No. For the Son of God, Jesus Christ, who was preached among you by us—by me, Silvanus, and Timothy—was not Yes and No, but in Him was Yes. For all the promises of God in Him are Yes, and in Him Amen, to the glory of God through us (2 Corinthians 1:17-20).

Not only does Paul confirm the principle of God's truthfulness and faithfulness, but he also declares that *all* of God's promises are still *yes* in Jesus!

Therefore, we have seen in this first chapter that God has in fact promised to restore the land of Israel, and that this is not a conditional or temporary promise. No, He will continue to bring it to pass even to a thousand generations and will fulfill it through Jesus to the endtimes. The trustworthiness of its fulfillment does not depend on any people—past, present, or future—but on the *nature* of the immutable God with whom it is impossible to lie. So if this God of truth raises His hand to signify the earnestness of His heart-given promise, we had better believe He means it and will do exactly as He says. *We cannot mute God!*

GOD IS FAITHFUL!

Chapter 2

I Will Multiply Men

Theologians make a serious mistake when they lightly dismiss Israel on the basis of her sin—even though God has referred to this sin historically as profane and adulterous behavior. This mistake is like a space probe that is sent off at an error of only one degree, but that misses its mark by millions of miles at the other end of its mission. The angle of error is a constant, but the distance from the desired course grows wider the farther away the probe travels from the genesis point. We are talking about a very critical and fundamental aspect of God's plan. Does His purpose turn on the whims and vagaries of man? Does He discard plans and blueprints like some cosmic mad scientist? Certainly the Scriptures reveal individual judgment, but God is able to judge between the unrepentant and the repentant within the same family. In this chapter we deal with the people of promise in Ezekiel 36. God will restore their place in the end.

The Issue

The issue, therefore, is not the state of individual Jews, or even generations of rebellion, but the covenant oath of the immutable, unchangeable God. There is no doubt that a strong case could be made for the sins of the Jewish people. They have certainly sinned against God, but of course, this is true for all of us. "For all have sinned and fall short of the glory of God" (Rom. 3:23). Also, Romans 3:10 says, "As it is written: 'there is none righteous, no, not one.' " This is a quotation taken directly from the Old Testament:

The fool has said in his heart, "There is no God." They are corrupt, and have done abominable iniquity; there is none who does good. God looks down from heaven upon the children of men, to see if there are any who understand, who seek God. Every one of them has turned aside; they have together become corrupt; there is none who does good, no, not one (Psalm 53:1-3).

The issue is not who will behave or who won't behave, but "What has God said?" The ultimate outcome is based on the character and ability of the One who promised. To focus on the object of His love instead of the *source* of that love in His loving nature, is the error of one degree that causes us to miss the point by a million miles. Therefore, the reason I have certain real expectations regarding the land and people of Israel is *not* because of their behavior, but because of His oath. The entire infrastructure of the Scriptures depends absolutely upon the veracity of the One who spoke it. If God's oath in Ezekiel 36 has been broken, or ever will be revoked, then we have no basis for believing anything He says! If the One who gave that oath could break it, then we who hope in salvation through Jesus are hoping in vain. If God is a covenant breaker—even if just one time—then His absolute nature of faithfulness is compromised, and His word cannot logically be trusted on any point. I know this is a hard word, but it is critical to our faith.

I Will Multiply Men

Do you see my point? The truthful God cannot lie! "God is not a man, that He should lie, nor a son of man, that He should repent. Has He said, and will He not do? Or has He spoken, and will He not make it good?" (Num. 23:19)

God faithfully "keeps covenant and mercy for a thousand generations" (Deut. 7:9). Again in Psalm 105:8-10 the Word says, "He remembers His covenant forever, The word which He commanded, for a thousand generations, the covenant which He made with Abraham, and His oath to Isaac, and confirmed it to Jacob for a statute, to Israel as an everlasting covenant." Another important principle is expressed in this passage: "For I am the Lord. I speak, and the word which I speak will come to pass; it will no more be postponed; for in your days, O rebellious house, I will say the word and perform it..." (Ezek. 12:25). This means that God not only speaks the word, but He is also the One who makes it happen! At some point in history (which someone has succinctly defined as "His-story"), God will bring about the precise fulfillment of His promise. It is God who speaks a word and it is God who will bring it to pass. The exact manner and *timing* of His word being fulfilled may well be debatable. But the *fact* of it is as sure as the God who said it. We may not like it, but we had better not try to tinker with the preordained intentions of the Creator. If we do, we will find ourselves as off course as that space probe mentioned earlier.

The divine nature of God is unchangeable. The prophet Malachi links that fact to the continued existence of the descendants of Jacob: "For I am the Lord, I do not change; therefore you are not consumed, O sons of Jacob" (Mal. 3:6). He is teaching them that if it were up to their behavior, God would have wiped them out! The only reason He has not is He gave

His word to their fathers. This divine characteristic is also seen in reference to Jesus: "Jesus Christ is the same yesterday, today, and forever" (Heb. 13:8). It is reinforced again in the Book of James. "Every good gift and every perfect gift is from above, and comes down from the Father of lights, with whom there is no variation or shadow of turning" (Jas. 1:17). There is *no variation* or *shadow* of *turning* with God! He will never deviate one degree from the precise foreordained destiny of purpose not only for Israel, but for all creation.

A Rebellious Nation

Ezekiel the prophet was called to his ministry with a mandate to speak the Lord's message whether or not the people received:

> *Then the Spirit entered me when He spoke to me, and set me on my feet; and I heard Him who spoke to me. And He said to me: "Son of man, I am sending you to the children of Israel, to a rebellious nation that has rebelled against Me; they and their fathers have transgressed against Me to this very day. For they are impudent and stubborn children. I am sending you to them, and you shall say to them, 'Thus says the Lord God.' As for them, whether they hear or whether they refuse—for they are a rebellious house—yet they will know that a prophet has been among them"* (Ezekiel 2:2-5).

They will know that "a prophet has been among them"! God delights in revealing His plans. His people—then or now—may not heed His warnings, but God will always raise up prophets to declare His truth.

Multiplication

Now, back to our study of Ezekiel 36, which we left in the middle of the passage of the prophet's message to the land.

I Will Multiply Men

This emphasis does not end in verse 8, but continues on through verse 15—at which point his prophecy is extended to include the *people* of the land. Although he still speaks to the land in verses 8-15, several references are made about the people: "they are about to come" (v. 8); "I will multiply men upon you" (v. 10); "I will multiply upon you man and beast; and they shall increase and bear young; I will make you inhabited as in former times, and do better for you than at your beginnings" (v. 11); and "Yes, I will cause men to walk on you, My people Israel; they shall take possession of you, and you shall be their inheritance; no more shall you bereave them of children" (v. 12).

Remember that the personal pronoun "you" in each of these verses refers to the land. God links the restoration of the people of Israel to keeping His covenant with the land of Israel. This prophecy has never been fulfilled and thus remains for these last days. We know it is talking about this final time of regathering because of the finality in key words used throughout the chapter, such as "no more," "anymore," "scattered," and "dispersed." Also, over and over he uses the plural, "nations" and "countries," as well as "*all* countries," which is a very significant clue. This cannot refer to the other historical captivities where Israel was taken each time to a specific single nation, as in the cases of Egypt and Babylon. The only restoration of Israel that fits the language of Ezekiel 36 is the great scattering or Diaspora of the two millennia since Jesus' earthly ministry. The outcasts of Israel have in historical fact been scattered to all the nations only in this final dispersion. The previous judgments each featured capture and exile to a single country. However, beginning with the era of the Roman Empire and in every generation since then till the present, they have been literally scattered among all the nations.

Prophesy to the Land

It is also important to note that they managed to maintain a Jewish identity during the 2000 years. No matter how assimilated they tried to become, they were still Jews. A contemporary paradox illustrates this point. In Israel, the rules spelling out who is a Jew can get rather technical and it often becomes a debatable issue. Some of the Russian Jews now fleeing to Israel are finding it difficult to prove that they are Jews. Yet in Russia there is no such debate. Every Russian Jew has a "J" stamped on his identity papers, which leads to serious problems of anti-Semitic discrimination and persecution. How ironic that Jews suffering so much at the hands of the Russian officials are then challenged as to their "Jewishness" when they arrive in the Promised Land! (There are, of course, some legitimate security concerns for Israel in avoiding infiltration. There are also financial reasons for the Israelis to be careful about admitting new immigrants, since every legitimate Jew is given a substantial monetary subsidy.)

Beginning in verse 16 of Ezekiel 36, the Lord gives another prophecy to the man of God, this time for the people. These verses will be explained more in the following chapter. However, there are a few more verses to examine now in the light of God's multiplying of men. First is verse 24: "For I will take you from among the nations, gather you out of all countries, and bring you into your own land." Verse 28 says, "Then you shall dwell in the land that I gave to your fathers; you shall be My people, and I will be your God." The chapter ends with this beautiful and profound promise in verses 37-38:

Thus says the Lord God: "I will also let the house of Israel inquire of Me to do this for them: I will increase their men like a flock. Like a flock offered as holy sacrifices, like the flock at Jerusalem on its feast days, so shall the ruined cities be filled with flocks of men. Then they shall know that I am the Lord" (Ezekiel 36:37-38).

I am an eyewitness to this phenomena. Each time I return to visit Israel, there are more people! The increase in population of a half million people in the past few years would be like the United States receiving 30 million new immigrants in the same period. In 1990 I had the privilege of speaking to a Messianic congregation in Tiberias that had just grown from 260 to 300 (mostly Israeli) believers by the addition of 40 Russian Pentecostal Jews who had recently obtained their citizenship. What joy we shared as their Siberian pastor, who could speak no English, hugged and kissed my neck, an American pastor who could speak no Russian! It was truly a foretaste of Divine glory.

GOD IS FAITHFUL!

Chapter 3

No Plan B

Was God surprised and taken off guard when Adam and Eve fell into sin? Did that event throw a monkey wrench into God's "little earth experiment"? Did He wring His hands and worry: "What am I going to do? Oh! What am I going to do now? I wasn't prepared for this!" Does God have a Plan A and B and perhaps a Plan C or D? Of course it sounds foolish when put this way, but has God ever been surprised by any development of history? This is a very critical and basic issue. This question is also pertinent to our whole story. If God just tries a plan "to see if it works" and in fact does not really know whether it will, then He is not the God of the Bible.

Remember the former things of old, for I am God, and there is no other; I am God, and there is none like Me, declaring the end from the beginning, and from ancient times things that are not yet done, saying, "My counsel shall stand, and I will do all My pleasure," calling a bird of prey from the east, the man who executes My counsel, from a far country. Indeed I have spoken it; I will also bring it to pass. I have purposed it; I will also do it (Isaiah 46:9-11).

This hardly sounds like one who is ruling at the whims of mankind's vacillating will. We do have a free will as it affects our personal place in God's plan, but our choices will neither alter nor thwart God's purpose. He is the only One who knows the outcome from beginning to end before it happens! "Declaring the end from the beginning, and from ancient times things that are not yet done, saying, 'My counsel shall stand, and I will do all My pleasure' " (Is. 46:10). There is no Plan B!

Some Christians today are actually being tempted by fleshly pride with the so-called "replacement theology" that says it didn't work out with Israel, so God raised up the Church to replace them. The real danger of this line of thinking is that if God could change His mind about all His promises to Israel, what would keep Him from changing His mind about the Church? Most people in the Western nations are ignorant of Islam, but Islamic theology teaches precisely that! They say Israel blew it and then God called the Church, but they blew it too, so God called Mohammed and the Muslims of Islam. In effect, they teach that Islam is Plan C. This is not true! *God does not revise His purpose to fit man, but He revises man to fit His purpose.* He has had only one plan from the beginning, and ultimately He will fulfill it, either with us or without us. In the end there will be an Israel fulfilling in exact literal detail every promise of the Bible, in concert with those promises to the Church in all nations.

The Old and New Covenants are a progressive revelation of the original blueprint. These testaments are not mutually exclusive or contradictory as some teach, but are a beautifully woven tapestry. They reveal the infinite artistry of our loving Creator who is revealed most perfectly in Jesus, the Alpha and the Omega, the beginning and the end. Jesus is not only the Omega of the New Testament, but He is also the Alpha of the Old Testament. God has been working on only one plan all along and it is right on schedule. Israel has always been in the plan and still is, even at the end. We, the Church, can only understand how we fit in the plan by understanding the context of Israel. The Church is grafted into Israel, the original planting of the Lord. There is no new tree! There is no Plan B!

Jesus was a Jew. The first apostles were Jewish. The early Church was Jewish. The drift away from our Jewish roots in Israel can be attributed to the success of evangelism. By sheer numbers, the believers are now overwhelmingly Gentile by birth and culture. But this does not cancel our Jewish roots. We will look more closely at the implications of this point in a later chapter when we analyze how the Jerusalem Council in Acts 15 had great bearing on our contemporary situation. If new Gentile believers were not required to be Judaized, then today's new Jewish believers should not be "Gentile-ized." We require far too much cultural conformity to non-biblical church traditions. Can a Jew remain culturally Jewish and still believe in Jesus? Does he have to "buy in" to all of our traditions? Is there a proper role for Messianic Judaism in contemporary Christianity?

Conditional vs. Unconditional Promises

Now, I recognize the difference between the types of promises. Sometimes God says that *if we* do this or that, then *He will* do such and such. However, the promises we are dealing with in this book have never been nullifed and will be precisely fulfilled. This fulfillment does not ignore Israel's sinful behavior; on the contrary, it includes the specific acknowledgment of her profane and "unacceptable" record. God does not imply that Israelites are not judged. He clearly *links* their scattering or Diaspora as the proper rejection and punishment.

> *Therefore I poured out My fury on them for the blood they had shed on the land, and for their idols with which they had defiled it. So I scattered them among the nations, and they were dispersed throughout the countries; I judged them according to their ways and their deeds* (Ezekiel 36:18-19).

He scattered them and judged them righteously because they deserved it.

Even in the dispersion, Israel continued to sin. This point is given five-fold emphasis in Ezekiel 36:20-23. The first occurs in verse 20: "wherever they went, they *profaned* My holy name". The second follows in verse 21: "But I had concern for My holy name, which the house of Israel had *profaned* among the nations wherever they went." Again, it says in verse 22, "My holy name's sake, which you have *profaned*," and finally it is mentioned twice (the fourth and fifth occurrences) in verse 23: "And I will sanctify My great name, which has been *profaned* among the nations, which you have *profaned* in their midst." The premise that Israel's sin could utterly remove her is contradictory to this passage of unconditional promise. If the promise depended upon Israel's behavior, she certainly would have been permanently rejected. But again and again in this passage and throughout the Bible, God expresses His mercy and grace based on His character alone. He will keep

His word. He is always faithful even when Israel, or we in the Church, are not.

Bypassed or Restored?

Another profound linkage is revealed in this passage. God first links their sin to their dispersion, but then He plainly links their regathering *not* to their behavior, but to His holy name! He must uphold the integrity of the promises He gave to their fathers. "I do not do this for your sake, O house of Israel, but for My holy name's sake…" (Ezek. 36:22). Again in verse 32 it says, " 'Not for your sake do I do this,' says the Lord God, 'let it be known to you. Be ashamed and confounded for your own ways, O house of Israel!' " But God's great plan will be fulfilled not in *bypassing* them, but by *saving* them. That is the miracle that reveals the glory of God.

And I will sanctify My great name, which has been profaned among the nations, which you have profaned in their midst; and the nations shall know that I am the Lord," says the Lord God, *"when I am hallowed in you before their eyes"* (Ezekiel 36:23).

The *nations* will know God is Lord *when* He is considered holy or hallowed by Israel in front of the nations. This truly is the amazing grace of the faithful God. The apostle Paul saw this promise also: "For if their being cast away is the reconciling of the world, what will their acceptance be but life from the dead?" (Rom. 11:15) There is no Plan B.

Ezekiel 36 lists many unconditional promises, and some are very specific. As we continue reading in verse 24, the Lord indicates that the regathering of the people of Israel to the land of Israel will be followed by a supernatural work of God in

them. God says He will do *seven supernatural works* to restore them to relationship with Him in verses 25-26:
1. He will "sprinkle clean water" on them (which I take to indicate the outpouring of the Holy Spirit).
2. He will "cleanse" them from "filthiness."
3. He will "cleanse" them from "all idols."
4. He will "give" them "a new heart."
5. He will "put a new spirit within" them.
6. He will remove their "heart of stone."
7. He will give them "a heart of flesh."

I will put My Spirit within you and cause you to walk in My statutes, and you will keep My judgments and do them. Then you shall dwell in the land that I gave to your fathers; you shall be My people, and I will be your God. I will deliver you from all your uncleannesses... (Ezekiel 36:27-29).

This supernatural personal restoration leads to their permission to dwell in the land in this restored relationship with God, complete with seven more specific *blessings* in verses 29-31.
1. Multiplied grain.
2. No famine.
3. Multiplied fruit.
4. Increased harvest in their fields.
5. Never again bear the reproach of nations due to famine.
6. Remembrance of evil ways. (I see this as a blessing because those who forget the mistakes of history are destined to repeat those mistakes.)

7. Self-loathing. (This is the recognition of the nature of unredeemed man and is a necessary prerequisite leading to repentance and salvation.)

One More List

Finally, lest we be tempted in any way to spiritualize this passage and these promises, He brings us back to the land in verse 33. The theme at the start of Ezekiel 36 was the land, and the prophecy ends with *seven blessings on the land*!

1. The cities and ruins will be rebuilt.
2. The land will be tilled.
3. The desolate land will be like the garden of Eden.
4. The cities will be fortified.
5. The cities will be inhabited.
6. The nations will know that it was the Lord who did the rebuilding.
7. The cities will be filled with flocks of men.

God tells the prophet Ezekiel in verse 36 to prophesy in the first person, speaking for God: "I, the Lord, have spoken it, and I will do it." then finally in verse 38 he says for God, "Then they shall know that I am the Lord." There is an unmistakable aspect of this story that, by necessity, includes the prophetic voice of God. I believe that there is destined to be a great revival harvest of lost souls at the end of the age. Much of it will result from the people of God today lifting up their voices to prophesy the word of the Lord. There are certainly very specific restraints and protections given in Scripture about how to judge contemporary prophecies but the rules are not given to eliminate the prophetic declarations, but to set them apart. If God's intention was to eliminate the gifts, there would have been no point in including such specific rules in the Bible such as 1 Corinthians 12–14. God is still speaking through His prophetic voice today by the power and manifestation of His Holy Spirit. We should rejoice for the current revival. However, not all are happy about what God is doing with Israel….

GOD IS FAITHFUL!

Chapter 4

Is the Church Becoming Anti-Semitic Again?

A new wave of anti-Israel theology is gaining credibility in the United States. These beliefs have raised some controversial questions about Israel, shaking the theology of many American Christians. Some go so far as to deny the scope or even the historical fact of the Holocaust. Under the banner of "replacement theology," these doctrines reiterate some of the heresies that many of us hoped had died in that World War II bunker with Adolph Hitler and his "solution to the Jewish problem."

In his book *To Whom Is God Betrothed?* Earl Paulk, Jr., purports to discuss "the Biblical basis for the church's support of national Israel," but instead proceeds to detail why he believes the Church should *not* support the nation of Israel today.(1) He uses Scripture to defend his case, but in my opinion, he misuses the Bible to once again give homage to tired old arguments that would be better left in the Dark Ages.

Three topics in particular deserve to be examined: (a) Do the Jews *alone* hold the guilt for killing Jesus Christ? (b) Did God thereafter divorce His Jewish bride and marry the Church as a second wife? (c) Is God through with Israel today as a chosen, unique covenant people?

The heresy suggested in these three questions may not be immediately apparent to all, so allow me to explain. The first question of Israel's singular guilt potentially undermines our basic doctrine of sin. The next issue of the two brides would have God as a polygamist or have God divorcing a first wife and marrying a different bride. The third issue questions the nature of God as the One who *keeps* His covenants. These ideas are challenges to biblical orthodoxy.

Are the Jews Alone Responsible?

Look closely at the first question. Are the Jews *alone* responsible for Jesus' death? One of the most heinous charges throughout history has been the self-righteous and arrogant epithet "Christ-Killers!" that was hurled at Jews during the Crusades, the Spanish Inquisition, and Hitler's holocaust. Even today in the inner cities of any metropolitan area around the world where Israel has been scattered, young Gentiles still mock and spit upon young Hebrew boys for the same reason. Jews are one of many ethnic groups that suffer prejudice, but they are unique in the religious basis of the abuse. They are victims of a generalized condemnation of an entire people group as being responsible for killing the world's Savior. No single person can defend himself from such an absolute judgment.

But the question remains, and deserves an honest answer: Are the Jews alone the ones who killed Jesus? What do the Scriptures teach? Consider what the company of believers prayed in Acts 4:27 upon the release of Peter and John. Having ealier quoted Psalm 2, which itself implicates the Gentiles (nations), the prayer to God continues: "For truly against Your holy Servant Jesus, whom You anointed, both Herod and Pontius Pilate, with the Gentiles and the people of Israel, were gathered together to do whatever Your hand and Your purpose determined before to be done" (Acts 4:27-28).

There are two undeniable facts stated here. First, *both Jew and Gentile* killed Christ. Second, it was the purpose of God! Paul warns Gentiles in Romans 11:18 when speaking of the Jewish branch temporarily broken off: "Do not boast against the branches...." Continuing in verses 20-21 he warns further: "...Do not be haughty, but fear. For if God did not spare the natural branches, He may not spare you either." Some Christians would judge and punish the Jews, but nowhere in the Scriptures are we given that assignment. The sovereign God has reserved that right to Himself; He is the only One to vindicate His plan. He knows that we are all guilty before Him and His final word is this: "...Vengeance is Mine, I will repay, says the Lord" (Rom. 12:19). Our plea should be for mercy—for ourselves and for the Jewish people.

Did God Divorce Israel?

The second major question concerns the Bride of Christ. The "new wave" theology in question does not dispute the fact that Israel was God's wife in the Old Testament. They contend that God has broken His marriage covenant with His Jewish bride because of her unfaithfulness and sin. The notion says that God, having put away His first wife, is now preparing a new bride, which is the Church.

Yet Jesus says that Moses only permitted divorce "because of the hardness of your heart" (Mk. 10:5). God's heart is not hardened! Hosea reveals the classic illustration of God's heart toward Israel. The anti-Israel view has God divorcing Israel as Hosea divorced his adulterous wife. This view teaches that God permanently broke His covenant with Israel. This is not true. He turned away from her in judgment, but God did not divorce Israel and break the marriage covenant. Hosea did divorce Gomer, but the end of the story is overlooked. In the end, both Gomer and Israel are restored (see Hos. 2:14–3:5; 14). In every generation there have been literal descendants of Israel who have embraced this faith in God. God has always had a remnant no matter how small, and has thereby continually maintained His covenant in force. God is faithful even when we are not! He is able to save to the uttermost all those who call on Him! He is the Redeemer, the One who keeps His promises. Don't make Him like one of us. *God is not made in man's image.*

In Romans 11:26 Paul quotes Isaiah 59:20, saying God will yet keep His covenant with Israel to *"turn away ungodliness from Jacob"*! The name *Jacob* is used, so it is absolutely clear that God is talking about the natural Jewish descendants of Abraham.

> *And they also, if they do not continue in unbelief, will be grafted in, for God is able to graft them in again. For if you were cut out of the olive tree which is wild by nature, and were grafted contrary to nature into a cultivated olive tree, how much more will these, who are natural branches, be grafted into their own olive tree? For I do not desire, brethren, that you should be ignorant of this mystery, lest you should be wise in your own opinion, that blindness in part has happened to Israel until the fullness of the Gentiles has come in. And so all Israel will be saved, as it is written: "The*

Deliverer will come out of Zion, and He will turn away ungodliness from Jacob; for this is My covenant with them, when I take away their sins." Concerning the gospel they are enemies for your sake, but concerning the election they are beloved for the sake of the fathers. For the gifts and the calling of God are irrevocable (Romans 11:23-29).

The last verse, the great promise about God's gifts and calling being irrevocable, has been preached by many over the centuries and has been applied to a host of different situations: personal, family, church, denominational, and even national. However, the literal textual application of verse 29 is specifically applied to natural Israel. God has not permanently divorced her. She is destined to be forgiven and restored!

Why Does It Matter to Us?

Let us turn now to the third and final question. Why would the doctrine of the permanent rejection of national Israel threaten us? If God said He would keep His covenant to a thousand generations, (which He did in Psalm 105:7-11), then how good is God's word? If God could give promises to Israel and break them, then why should we be confident that He will keep His word to us? The very doctrine of the nature of God is at stake. Some may say "But, Jesus died for us and the Holy Spirit has sealed our salvation!" Of course this is true, but we know it and accept it by *faith*. What if God decided to change His mind? Could we appeal to Him to keep His word based on *our* character or works? Certainly not! For that matter, who could appeal to a God who could not be trusted?

Now do you see how unfounded and dangerous it is to suggest that God broke His covenant with Israel? God's very essence is that of a covenant keeper. It is man who cannot be trusted; "...let God be true but every man a liar" (Rom. 3:4a). Let us pray for the people of Israel that God would forgive their sins, open their eyes to Messiah Jesus, and totally restore them to their land and their God! Isaiah predicts the coming of Jesus as Messiah in Isaiah 11:10; in verse 11 he says that the Lord shall bring back Israel "the second time" and verse 12 he says they will be gathered "from the four corners of the earth"! This is now being fulfilled. Praise the Lord Jesus!

In Ezekiel's vision of the dry bones in chapter 37, he saw the bones come together *before* they received their life-breath. Israel is now being gathered as dry bones. Today's question is the same: "Can these bones live?" It is my deep conviction that we are living in the generation of the salvation of Israel. It has begun! For a full treatment of this subject, I heartily recommend the thrilling account of God's contemporary exploits written by Steve Lightle, entitled *Exodus II*.(2) Steve shares his own vision and experiences regarding the exodus of Jews from Russia and the rest of the former Soviet bloc, and tells of their return to the land of Israel.

If God supernaturally reveals Jesus as Messiah to Israel in these last days, what is the Church going to do? The answer is in the wisdom of Acts 15 where the council wrestled with "the Gentile problem." What were they going to do about Gentiles being saved? Did they need to be *Judaized*? You see, most believers then were Jews. The answer was a clear *no*. It was enough that they receive Jesus, avoid immorality, and abstain from idols. Today, almost all believers are Gentile and we are about to face the *same problem in reverse*. As more Jews are saved, we will have to face the question: Do Jews need to be "*Gentile-ized*" and become culturally Gentile in order to be saved? The wise answer once again will be *no*. It is enough that they receive Jesus as Messiah. They are *not pagans*, in the classic sense, if they worship the God of Abraham, Isaac, and Jacob. They do not need to renounce their God and convert to a "Christian God," but they do need to recognize that dependance upon the law is not a means of salvation. All who are saved in both Testaments are saved by faith as "[Abraham] did not waver at the promise of God through unbelief, but was strengthened in faith, giving glory to God, and being fully convinced that what He had promised He was also able to perform. And therefore 'it was accounted to him for righteousness' " (Rom. 4:20-22). "And he believed in the Lord and He accounted it to him for righteousness." (Gen. 15:6) Faith is believing God. He is the only God and Jesus is the only Messiah. *Jews do not need to renounce Judaism, but they must accept Jesus*, who said, "I am the way, the truth, and the life. No one comes to the Father except through Me" (Jn. 14:6). If you, dear reader, have not been saved, you simply need to turn from your sin and believe God's promise of forgiveness through Jesus the Messiah. It is God who saves. "For by grace you have been saved through faith, and that not of yourselves; it is the gift of God, not of works, lest anyone should boast" (Eph. 2:8-9). Why not talk to God yourself right now and settle this issue in your life for all eternity?

Pray for the Real Peace of Jerusalem!

We have seen in Part I of this book, "The Premise: The Faithfulness of God's Character." In Part II, we will take a look at "The Promise: The Faithfulness of God's Word."

GOD IS FAITHFUL!

Part II

The Promise: The Faithfulness of God's Word

Chapter 5

Nuts and Bolts

The promises of God are not haphazard, but orderly. They fit into the master blueprint by the preordained design of the Master Architect. Abraham "waited for the city which has foundations, whose builder and maker is God" (Heb. 11:10). "The steps of a good man are ordered by the Lord" (Ps. 37:23a).

The Bible is clear in presenting a God of order and design. The serious student of the Scriptures soon learns that there are certain principles which, when applied, will yield understanding. However, before we look at some of the faithful promises regarding Israel, let's look at what I call "nuts and bolts."

Consider these discussions as a guide to some of the presuppositional distinctions that have influenced my thinking and study. What are some of the pertinent principles and relevant concepts that fit into this category?

Prophecy vs. Prophesy

It is critical that we make a distinction between those two words in order to avoid confusion. We have already alluded to some comparisons in Part I of this book, such as conditional versus unconditional promises. Another that we mentioned earlier, but did not explain is the difference between prophecy and prophesy. The first is the noun referring to the *content* of God's message. The second is a verb relating to the *command* of God to speak the message. Thus the theme of this book invokes the latter use (as a verb), and quotes God's directive to Ezekiel to declare His prophetic word to the physical land.

Flesh vs. Flesh

One rather confusing word in the English translations of the Bible is the word *flesh*. There are two quite different uses of the same word.(1) The obvious first meaning is simply the physical body of man or the meat of animals. The second usage is a concept that is a little more complicated. Carnal behavior is considered to be "of the flesh." This use refers to the old sinful nature of man before redemption. In this context, "flesh" is the opposite of "spirit." "So then, those who are in the flesh cannot please God. But you are not in the flesh but in the Spirit, if indeed the Spirit of Christ dwells in you…" (Rom. 8:8-9). It is quite clear in this reference that Paul is not talking about the physical body, but about the carnal condition of man without God. If he were saying those in a physical body can't please God, we would have no hope until eternity. But the good news of the gospel teaches us that with the Holy Spirit in us, we *can* please God in this life by living according to the Spirit. Paul uses the other meaning of flesh in Romans 9:3-4: "For I could wish that I myself were accursed from Christ for my brethren, my countrymen according to the flesh, who are Israelites, to whom pertain the adoption, the glory, the covenants, the giving of the law, the service of God, and the promises." He is not using "flesh" as "carnal," but as "physical." It is important for us to understand this because when we see a verse that talks about promises to "Israel after the flesh," we must understand it is physical Israel and not carnal Israel that is given a promise. We can only figure out which of the opposing interpretations apply by studying the context in the specific passage and by comparing it with the overall teaching of Scripture to make sure there is real agreement.

Biblical Interpretation

If we are left with two possible ways of looking at a word or a verse, and the rest of the testimony of the Bible is clearly supportive of one view, then we conclude that the view being supported is the proper understanding of the specific passage in question. This principle is known as "interpreting Scripture by Scripture." The second principle is "interpreting Scripture by context." The actual scriptural evidence takes precedence over culture, non-biblical history, logic, and personal experience. We submit all our knowledge to the final authority of the Bible. This acceptance of the authority of Scripture as our objective standard of comparison is critical; it is the only basis on which I attempt to say anything in this book. There is a third interpretative principle that also needs mentioning. It is called the "double emphasis." When a word, verse, or concept is repeated, or mentioned numerous times in a passage, then it deserves special notice. A good example is the five-fold emphasis in Ezekiel 36 of the fact that Israel profaned God among the nations, which I pointed out in the previous section. When the Holy Spirit (who inspired the writers of the Bible) gives multiple emphasis, we need to sit up and take notice. For further in-depth study of biblical interpretation, I recommend these two excellent books: *Interpreting the Scriptures* by

Kevin Conner and Ken Malmin(2); and *Protestant Biblical Interpretation* by Bernard Ramm.(3)

Samson and the Palestinians

Some would think that analyzing words makes the Bible too complicated. On the contrary, such analysis has the effect of simplifying the Bible. I could have titled this chapter "Fun With Words," because it is entertaining to reduce obscure references to simple understanding. The "flesh versus flesh" distinction already mentioned is an example. Let's look at a few more.

For some unexplainable reason, many Bible translators use the words *Gentiles* and *nations* as though they were two different words. This is unfortunate because it adds to the confusion. They could use either word all the time, but by switching back and forth, they create the idea that nations and Gentiles are different. This is wrong. We must read either word with the idea that the other could be easily interchanged without harm to the context.

There is another set of words that is even more fun to meditate on: Philistine versus Palestinian. These words are not seen to be identical in English, but in Hebrew they are the same! It is very interesting to think of today's modern Palestinians in comparison with the Philistines of Samson's and David's times. These people have many similarities: enemies of Israel, terrorist raids on Israel, and the same geographical concentration (Gaza, West Bank, etc.), to name a few. Perhaps you see other parallels. It's fascinating to note that no less a modern figure than Yassar Arafat claims to be descended from the Philistines. Although this is a dubious possibility in the natural, he certainly manifests the same spirit. The Philistines were known more for terrorism than for a great army.

Literal vs. Spiritual

There is another distinction we need to make that will clear up a lot of confusion. Every Bible verse should be taken literally if there is any possible way to do so. This is our first priority in understanding any passage. In relatively rare cases there seems to be no possible literal meaning and we can only understand it as symbolic or spiritual. Many passages have both a literal and a spiritual meaning, and I am not opposed to seeing the spiritual application as long as we also allow the literal.

This is where the Church's idea of Israel becomes unnecessarily mixed up. We are so used to spiritualizing everything in claiming the promises for ourselves (we *are* grafted in, after all), that we tend to overlook the literal. Ezekiel 36:27 is a classic example. For many years I have claimed this promise of the Holy Spirit for myself, learning of its fulfillment in Acts 2 on the Day of Pentecost and seeing it personally in my own life in June 1968. It is good for us to see that we are grafted into the promises, but we must *allow* God to bring about the literal completion of His prophecy to Israel in the timing of Ezekiel 36, which is clearly linked to a scattering and regathering that had not occurred even on the Day of Pentecost. Perhaps Peter thought the outpouring in his day was the end, yet, 2000 years later we now see the "last days" of Acts 2 in the light of the rest of Joel 2 (from which Peter quoted and based his conclusion: "But this is what was spoken by the prophet Joel" [Acts 2:16]).

Joel saw the last days as compared to the seasons of Israel. These seasons include early rains followed by a growing season and ending with latter rains, greater than the early rains, that allowed the crops to ripen at harvest time. His analogy is precise: The outpouring of the Holy Spirit in the last days is comparable to the rainy seasons of Israel. I believe that this is an excellent model with which to view church history: the early rain of Pentecost, the dry time (corresponding to the Dark Ages), followed by the latter rain which refers to the outpouring we are witnessing in our day, the harvest time of history. Why is it so hard for some to include a restoration of physical Israel in this great end-time outpouring of the Holy Spirit? The Bible does teach it, if we now take literally passages that we had once consigned to the "symbolic only" category. Maybe it is time for some of us to reexamine our positions.

Dispensationalism or Sensationalism?

Dispensationalism is a prominent popular view of the Bible that we need to consider. We will take a brief overview of what pertains to our subject because there are so many different extremes of the dispensational method of biblical interpretation. This method can be dangerous since it usually involves devising an external (from Scripture) means of dividing the Bible into chronological sections, called dispensations. The trouble comes when we impose our prejudiced prior view on the Bible instead of letting the Bible tell us the correct view. A very dangerous assumption often made says that things relegated to one dispensation will not overlap into another time compartment; therefore, certain things may then be dispensed with. A clear example from our day is the controversy surrounding the gifts of the Holy Spirit, such as speaking in tongues. We simply create a neat little time box for it and say it was only for that time and not for today. Then we no longer have to deal with it either theologically or personally. With a little flick of our dispensational magic wand, it's gone! In reality it is not that easy. God does not like to be put in a box. Just when we think we have it all figured out, He blows up our boxes. God does not change and Jesus is the same forever, so there must be a limit to how far we go in creating such "time zones."

Law vs. Grace

There is a lot of overlapping of our neat little boxes and the best example is law versus grace. Nearly everyone agrees that the Old Testament was the "age of law" and the New Testament the "age of grace." However, let me ask a simple question: Were Old Testament people saved by keeping the law? No, they were saved by belief in Jesus (not knowing His name), by believing that God would send His Son, the Messiah, to save them. They were saved by looking ahead to Jesus' finished work on the cross. We are saved by looking back to that great sacrifice of the Lamb of God who took away the sins of the world. By the same token, did the law end at some point in time? No, it is still in effect for those who, being unrepentant, are not in grace. They will be judged according to the law, which reveals God's holy and righteous standards. The law is not canceled by Jesus, but is fulfilled in Him and through Him. Jesus said, "Do not think that I came to destroy the Law or the Prophets. I did not come to destroy but to fulfill. For assuredly, I say to you, till heaven and earth pass away, one jot or one tittle will by no means pass from the law till all is fulfilled" (Mt. 5:17-18). A jot is the smallest Hebrew letter and a tittle is the smallest stroke used in any Hebrew letter. That sounds like a profound point for Jesus to make. I don't think He was mistaken. Only those in grace are freed from the law; everyone else will be judged by the law and condemned by it. For a profound scholarly treatment of this subject, please refer to the monumental work by Rousas John Rushdoony. In his Introduction he develops this point: "The alternative to law is not grace; it is lawlessness."(4)

If you can fully grasp what I am saying, you'll understand how important it is to this book. People would like to put Israel in some neat little historical box, never to be heard from again. But God has a *plan* that He began and will fulfill. He intends to fulfill in natural Israel the promises He made to Israel's fathers. In the final analysis, God will do what He wants to do, or more precisely, He will do what He has always said He would do!

Hidden vs. Revealed

What is the advantage of having God reveal His truth to us? Would we be at a disadvantage if He not only declined to reveal the truth, but in fact actually hid it from us? Of course we would, and that is exactly the case with the Jewish people. Through the centuries, God certainly revealed Jesus to many individuals, but it has been very difficult for the remainder of the Jews because *God* blinded their eyes. I am not going to deal with the "fairness" of it—only the fact of it. God is righteous and merciful and that is all we need to know about His "fairness." But we must deal with the fact that God has blinded them. "...God has given them a spirit of stupor, eyes that they should not see And ears that they should not hear, to this very day" (Rom. 11:8). "For I do not desire, brethren, that you should be ignorant of this mystery, lest you should be wise in your own opinion, that blindness in part has happened to Israel until the fullness of the Gentiles has come in" (Rom. 11:25). Notice the word *until* in this verse; it is a timing word and indicates that this blinding of Israel has a limited duration, and then will be removed! (The topic of the times of the Gentiles is discussed at greater length in Chapter 20.) Yet even during the time of general blindness for Israel, any individual Jew could be saved if he or she sincerely called on the Lord. "But even to this day, when Moses is read, a veil lies on their heart. Nevertheless when one turns to the Lord, the veil is taken away" (2 Cor. 3:15-16). Please note that the phrase "even to this day" refers not to our day, but Paul's.

Israel vs. Judah

One final distinction should be made in our review of "nuts and bolts." Is there any difference between Israel and Judah or between Israelites and Jews? Yes, they were distinct during the time of the divided kingdoms. A little known fact, however, is that all of the tribes were still represented in the list of those returning from Babylon in the time of Nehemiah. The tribes are also listed in the Book of Revelation, so we understand that Israel was reunited. Therefore, having picked up the name *Jew* during the time of the kingdom of Ahasuerus following the return under Ezra and Nehemiah, the name has stuck and is now used interchangeably for all Israel. Today in Israel you would hear the term *Israeli*, while in other nations you would more likely hear the term *Jew*. An interesting footnote to history is the fact that when the Jews voted in 1948 on what to name their new nation, it was evenly divided and Israel just barely won over Judah. I believe *Israel* was chosen in the sovereignty of God as another piece of the puzzle coming into place to fulfill God's promise of Israel's restoration.

Even the promise of removing the veil of blindness is linked to the land.

> And in this *mountain*
> The Lord of hosts will make
> for all people
> A feast of choice pieces,
> A feast of wines on the lees,

Of fat things full of marrow,
Of well-refined wines on the lees.
And He will destroy on this *mountain*
The surface of the *covering* cast over all people.
And the *veil* that is spread over all nations.
He will swallow up death forever,
And the Lord God will wipe away tears from all faces;
The rebuke of His people
He will take away from all the earth;
For the Lord has spoken.
And it will be said in that day:
"Behold, this is our God;
We have waited for Him, and He will save us.
This is the Lord;
We have waited for Him;
We will be glad and rejoice in His salvation."
For on this *mountain* the hand of the Lord will rest…
(Isaiah 25:6-10).

GOD IS FAITHFUL!

Chapter 6

Prophesy to the Bones

Here we go again! Ezekiel hardly has time to recover from being sent out to talk to dirt, when God tells him to go prophesy to some bones! One of the most popular sermon passages in the Old Testament is Ezekiel 37. The prophet tells of his incredible vision of a valley full of dry bones in some country far from Israel. Usually, when this text is expounded, the application is made to the Church because of the beautiful promises of the Holy Spirit in verses 5, 9, 10, and 14. However, as we have indicated in the previous chapter in making the distinction between literal and spiritual, we must look at this text regarding what it says *literally* about natural Israel.

"Can these bones live?" is the question that dominates the message of this chapter. God asked it of Ezekiel, who replied, "O Lord God, You know" (Ezek. 37:3). This picture is a prophetic vision as suggested in verse 1: "The hand of the Lord came upon me and brought me out in the Spirit of the Lord, and set me down in the midst of the valley; and it was full of bones." It was such an incredible scene of death—only bones were left and they were very dry, implying that they had been dead a long time. The prospect of their coming back to life was obviously impossible. Yet when God is the One asking, you have to allow for anything, so Ezekiel left it with God. It was a wise answer because God immediately continued with the prophecy He wanted spoken to the bones:

Again He said to me, "Prophesy to these bones, and say to them, 'O dry bones, hear the word of the Lord! Thus says the Lord God to these bones: "Surely I will cause breath to enter into you, and you shall live. I will put sinews on you and bring flesh upon you, cover you with skin and put breath in you; and you shall live. Then you shall know that I am the Lord" ' " (Ezekiel 37:4-6).

It is interesting to note that as the prophet obeyed the command, it happened just as the Lord said—*except* the breath did not come into them, even though the bones came together with sinews, flesh and skin. This is an indication that in applying this prophecy to the regathering of Israel in the last days, it may be quite complete before the "breath" comes upon them. Of course, I believe the breath represents the Holy Spirit regeneration, which is the only hope of life. Jesus is the best example of this as John 20:22 shows: "And when He had said this, He breathed on them, and said to them 'Receive the Holy Spirit.' "

Holocaust!

In Ezekiel 37:11, God says, "Son of man, these bones are the whole house of Israel. They indeed say, 'Our bones are dry, our hope is lost, and we ourselves are cut off!' " This is a picture of Israel in these last days when there seems to be no hope for spiritual life. The holocaust of World War II created a picture very similar to the vision of dry bones seen by the prophet.

If you have seen any actual film footage of that great atrocity, you can only shake your head in wonder that such a holocaust could ever occur. You can almost understand the temptation for future generations to try and deny that it ever happened. That is one way to avoid facing the hideous truth! But it did happen. It is fully documented that *six million Jews* and *five million Christians*, who were civilians, died at the hands of the German insanity. At the end of the war, when the United States Armed Forces discovered the concentration camps, they had all the troops in areas near the camps tour the horrible scenes. Soldiers were told to bring their own cameras to help record the awful truth so that no one would ever be able to deny that it happened. One of those young soldiers was Lawrence Fuller, my wife's uncle. Since he was an eyewitness of the Holocaust, I have included his account as a chapter titled simply, "Tears." This is a small contribution to the collective memory of that event—to honor the memory of the dead and to ensure that the living will never allow it to reoccur.

You Shall Know

Three times in Ezekiel 37, God follows His action with the statement: "Then you shall know that I am the Lord." First He brings the bones together with sinews, flesh, and skin; then He gives them the breath of life, and finally, He brings them back to the land. This marvelous working of God encourages the people of Israel to once again know God. Thus, the physical restoration of Israel is always taught in the context of their salvation. When I speak of Israel's salvation, I mean nothing less than receiving Jesus as Messiah, Lord and Son of God. The Bible clearly declares there is no other salvation: "Jesus said to him, 'I am the way, the truth, and the life. No one comes to the

Father except through Me' " (Jn. 14:6). "Nor is there salvation in any other, for there is no other name under heaven given among men by which we must be saved" (Acts 4:12).

Back to the Land

Let us return to Ezekiel 37:9 and think a little more about the breath. After the bones come together without life, the prophet is then instructed to "Prophesy to the breath, prophesy, son of man, and say to the breath, 'Thus says the Lord God: "Come from the four winds, O breath, and breathe on these slain, that they may live" ' " (Ezek. 37:9). Then, God says He will "cause you to come up from your graves, and bring you into the land of Israel" (Ezek. 37:12). Some believe this refers to the literal resurrection of all the dead at the second coming of Jesus, but I disagree because of the reference to the land and the context of Israel's restoration. There is also an amazingly similar analogy in Paul's teaching on the restoration of Israel: "For if their being cast away is the reconciling of the world, what will their acceptance be but life from the dead?" (Rom. 11:15) I am convinced that the return of the *people* of Israel to the *land* of Israel and the resurrection of the Jewish state on the world scene is a clear sign of the end. The whole world had considered the nation of Israel dead! In fact, it *was* dead for almost 2000 years! The miracle of her life again is confounding to most. We should once again take up the responsibility of Ezekiel and in sincere prophetic prayer speak to the breath to come and fill the regathered bones of God's people Israel.

When God puts His Holy Spirit in them, they will know the Lord again: " 'I will put My Spirit in you, and you shall live, and I will place you in your own land. Then you shall know that I, the Lord, have spoken it and performed it,' says the Lord" (Ezek. 37:14). This is the end of the first half of Ezekiel 37, but the second half has a related prophecy.

One Kingdom; One King

Since God never likes to leave loose ends, He wants to make one thing perfectly clear. The division of Israel at the time of the northern and southern kingdoms will not prevail in the end. Israel will once again be a nation in unity. The prophet is given another peculiar assignment in the second half of chapter 37 to pick up two sticks and write: "Judah" on one and "Israel" on the other. Then God continues:

Then join them one to another for yourself into one stick, and they will become one in your hand. ... say to them, "Thus says the Lord God: 'Surely I will take the stick of Joseph, which is in the hand of Ephraim, and the tribes of Israel, his companions; and I will join them with it, with the stick of Judah, and make them one stick, and they will be one in My hand.' " ...Then say to them "Thus says the Lord God: 'Surely I will take the children of Israel from among the nations, wherever they have gone, and will gather them from every side and bring them into their own land; and I will make them one nation in the land, on the mountains of Israel; and one king shall be king over them all; they shall no longer be two nations, nor shall they ever be divided into two kingdoms again' " (Ezekiel 37:17,19,21-22).

(The translation of the Hebrew word for *one* in the joining of the two sticks is the word *echad*, and has great significance in witnessing to Jewish people. Please refer to Chapter 10 for the explanation of *echad* and *yachid*. It will clear up confusion in the minds of Jewish people with regard to God's being "one.")

Still in Ezekiel 37, in verses 22-23 and 25-28, the prophecy uses timing words eight times to reveal the duration of this miracle of God. These eight words in order are: no longer, ever, anymore, forever, forever, everlasting, forevermore, and forevermore! Do you seriously think that this prophecy could possibly refer to some previous regathering of Israel? On the other hand, isn't it clearly predicting a final return that will *never* be revoked? By the way, the reference to "My servant David" in verse 25 is to Jesus, who is called the son of David and who will rule on the throne of David.

> *Then they shall dwell in the land that I have given to Jacob My servant, where your fathers dwelt; and they shall dwell there, they, their children, and their children's children, forever; and My servant David shall be their prince forever. Moreover I will make a covenant of peace with them, and it shall be an everlasting covenant with them; I will establish them and multiply them, and I will set My sanctuary in their midst forevermore. My tabernacle also shall be with them; indeed I will be their God, and they shall be My people. The nations also will know that I, the Lord, sanctify Israel, when My sanctuary is in their midst forevermore* (Ezekiel 37:25-28).

There is nothing hidden or secretive about this great restoration because the *nations will know*! This is why I take Ezekiel 37 literally. God has a beautiful plan for Israel which He will accomplish in full view of all the nations right on schedule just as He has promised throughout the Bible. However, the nations also have a plan revealed by God, as we shall see in the next chapter.

GOD IS FAITHFUL!

Chapter 7

World History Time Line

The twentieth Century has seen a remarkable phenomena catch the attention of Bible scholars around the world. The rise of various forms of dispensationalism has created confusion by adding unnecessary complexity to the study of Scripture. Allow me to submit a simple outline of history that permits the ready comprehension of prophecy, thus unlocking the Old Testament.

We begin with a profoundly simple premise: The scriptural view of history is always linear. The worldly view sees a parade of continuously repeating cycles with no creation and no conclusion. I submit that the Bible gives us a consolidated view that reports history as a series of meaningful events along a time line from a God-ordained origin to a God-enacted finale. The Bible, therefore, exists as His revelation and explanation of these events. "Surely the Lord does nothing, unless He reveals His secret to His servants the prophets" (Amos 3:7). Admittedly, there are certain aspects of God's purpose that are revealed in a progressively unfolding manner, but to radically dispensationalize history is to lose the unity of God's purpose.

For example, law and grace are often separated into opposite compartments of history. Yet in reality, both law and grace overlap their respective time compartments. No Old Testament hero is saved in any other manner than through the grace of God because he looked forward to and believed in the promised Messiah. To be more precise, these people believed the words of God who promised the Savior. Likewise in this so-called "age of grace" in which we live, the wicked will still be judged according to the law of God, for it still stands witness against all who live ungodly lives and who reject Jesus, the only true Messiah. "For the wrath of God is revealed from heaven against all ungodliness and unrighteousness of men, who suppress the truth in unrighteousness" (Rom. 1:18).

The neat and tidy division of even the most basic form of dispensationalism sounds better on paper than when applied in real life. God just does not fit into our boxes. If we keep trying to make Him fit into our explanations, we will grow more and more frustrated. It is much better to listen to His Word and repeat it to a thirsty world. One of the most remarkable teachings of the Gospel of John is a point that the writer makes over and over: Jesus did not initiate anything from Himself. He did what the Father wanted Him to do at all times and said what the Father wanted Him to say at all times. He did this perfectly and never once lapsed into His own selfwill. "Then Jesus answered and said to them, 'Most assuredly, I say to you, the Son can do nothing of Himself, but what He sees the Father do; for whatever He does, the Son also does in like manner' " (Jn. 5:19). I can of Myself do nothing. As I hear, I judge; and My judgment is righteous, because I do not seek My own will but the will of the Father who sent Me" (Jn. 5:30; see also Jn. 6:38; 8:28; 12:49; 14:10). Therefore, we should submit to the view the Bible gives regarding world history. We should view it from God's perspective, not man's.

Daniel's Image

The most consolidated historical viewpoint comes, not surprisingly, from the Scriptures themselves in the Book of Daniel. There a remarkable incident occured that has proven its uncanny accuracy by the indisputable test of time. This event takes place in the kingdom of Babylon, the first worldwide empire. As recorded in Daniel 2, King Nebuchadnezzar had an amazing dream that nobody could interpret for him. Of course, he made it rather difficult when he demanded that they not only tell the interpretation, but also the dream. None of his magicians, astrologers, or sorcerers could do such a thing, so Nebuchadnezzar decided to have them all executed. Considered to be a part of these were some wise Hebrew men, including Daniel who had been brought to Babylon when Judah and Jerusalem were conquered. Daniel, with his friends, began to seek the mercies of God for the secret so they would not be killed with the others. God answered Daniel and gave him a night vision of the dream and its interpretation.

Daniel's first statement to the king declares the two-fold purpose of the dream: "But there is a God in heaven who reveals secrets, and He has made known to King Nebuchadnezzar what will be in the latter days..." (Dan. 2:28). First, there is a God in Heaven who reveals secrets; and second, this secret holds a great key to the future of the world. It was a secret before Daniel received the interpretation, but not after!

God revealed the secret of His purpose for the nations of the world.

Thus, this great passage of Daniel becomes the outline of history. There would be five great world empires beginning with Babylon the Great and followed by four others in a clearly descending order of inferiority. "But after you shall arise another kingdom inferior to yours; then another, a third kingdom of bronze, which shall rule over all the earth" (Dan. 2:39). The second empire would be the divided Medo-Persian Empire; it would be followed by Alexander the Great's Greek Empire as the third; then the fourth would arise, the Roman Empire, divided between East and West as the image's legs. If you have some knowledge of history, I think it is quite clear that the first four empires are as I have outlined them. Remember that the Roman system, which had ruled the world with a rod of iron, was divided with two capitals: Rome and Constantinople. "And the fourth kingdom shall be as strong as iron, inasmuch as iron breaks in pieces and shatters everything; and like iron that crushes, that kingdom will break in pieces and crush all the others" (Dan. 2:40). It is well documented that Imperial Rome ruled with an iron fist, militarily.

Iron and Clay

Finally, the fifth world government seen by Daniel represents today's two great world systems of East and West, symbolized by the iron and clay of the toes of Daniel's image. These final kingdoms are described in Daniel 2:42-43:

And as the toes of the feet were partly of iron and partly of clay, so the kingdom shall be partly strong and partly fragile. As you saw iron mixed with ceramic clay, they will mingle with the seed of men; but they will not adhere to one another, just as iron does not mix with clay."

We have seen the emergence of these two systems in our lifetime. After World War II, the United States and the Soviet Union assumed their roles as the superpowers of the endtimes. The two great leaders at that critical juncture of historical emergence were President Dwight D. Eisenhower and Soviet Premier Nikita Khrushchev. The literal meaning of these two leaders' last names is an intriguing confirmation that God was at work in history: *Eisenhower* in German means "worker with iron" and Khrushchev in Ukrainian means "clay"!(1) This is one of those minute details of God's Word that reveals the magnificence of the true God who authored it through chosen men of God: "knowing this first, that no prophecy of Scripture is of any private interpretation, for prophecy never came by the will of man, but holy men of God spoke as they were moved by the Holy Spirit" (2 Pet. 1:20-21).

The amazing events in Russia and Eastern Europe at the turn of the last decade were exciting evidence of how close we are to the end. The Soviet Union, the weaker of the two final powers, is represented by clay in Daniel's vision, and has already disintegrated. Can the Western powers continue much longer? Economic realities say, "No!" There is also another phenomenal event taking place: The second great exodus of history is underway in Russia and Eastern Europe. More than 500,000 Russians have immigrated to Israel in the last few years.

"Therefore behold, the days are coming," says the Lord, "that it shall no more be said, 'The Lord lives who

brought up the children of Israel from the land of Egypt,' but, *'The Lord lives who brought up the children of Israel from the land of the **north and from all the lands** where He had driven them.' For I will bring them back into their land which I gave to their fathers"* (Jeremiah 16:14-15).

The Eternal Kingdom

The next kingdom of Daniel's prophecy is the last, and is not part of the image:

And in the days of these kings the God of heaven will set up a kingdom which shall never be destroyed; and the kingdom shall not be left to other people; it shall break in pieces and consume all these kingdoms, and it shall stand forever. Inasmuch as you saw that the stone was cut out of the mountain without hands, and that it broke in pieces the iron, the bronze, the clay, the silver, and the gold—the great God has made known to the king what will come to pass after this. The dream is certain, and its interpretation is sure (Daniel 2:44-45).

This is the eternal kingdom of God ruled by His Son, King Jesus! I would just like to point out two observations from this reference. One is that the victory is so total as to bring a final end to the five humanistic empires that evidently will all still have remnants left until the end. Second, it is notable that there is not a kingdom period allotted to any other kingdom, including that of the antichrist. Whatever temporary power he obtains, it is not even a dot on God's world history outline! Jesus is the Victor!

The significance of the continuity of historical events is not in the various kingdoms, but in the God who Himself orders all the events of history. God is the same throughout history! His purpose is revealed from the beginning in Genesis, with a Savior and a people. In the next chapter we will examine the people He works with to understand His purpose and to recognize the Savior.

GOD IS FAITHFUL!

Chapter 8

The Fall and Rising of Israel

Throughout history nations formed, rose to their highest levels of glory on the world scene, and then declined to a level of unimportance or disappeared altogether. Our review of world history in the last chapter is a classic example. Yet there is a fascinating prophecy given over the baby Jesus that amazingly contradicts the normal pattern, and is the subject of this chapter as it relates to Israel.

"Then Simeon blessed them, and said to Mary His mother, 'Behold, this Child is destined for the *fall and rising* of many in Israel, and for a sign which will be spoken against' " (Lk. 2:34). This verse has been overlooked by many scholars, but it hides a profound hint of revelation. Virtually every nation in the history of planet Earth follows the simple pattern of "rise and fall" except Israel! Most nations rise and fall, but Israel, which was falling in the time of Jesus, was destined to rise again. Even more to the point is the fact that Jesus Himself was destined to preside over both the *fall* of Israel in His first advent and then at its *rise* in His second coming! He was here to preside over the *fall* of Israel in the first century A.D. and He will return to preside over the resurrection of Israel at the end of time. "For if their being cast away is the reconciling of the world, what will their acceptance be but life from the dead?" (Rom. 11:15)

The Fall of Israel

Jesus accurately predicted the fall of Israel:

But when you see Jerusalem surrounded by armies, then know that its desolation is near. ... And they will fall by the edge of the sword, and be led away captive into all nations. And Jerusalem will be trampled by Gentiles until the times of the Gentiles are fulfilled (Luke 21:20,24).

The fall of Jerusalem was historically fulfilled in A.D. 70 as the Romans conquered Israel and began a long succession of Gentile rule in the Holy City, which finally ended in 1967 when Israel recaptured Jerusalem during the Six Day War.

Some of the greatest lessons of history are recorded in volumes of books about the rise and fall of empires. We studied the rise and fall of Babylon, the Medo-Persian empire, the Greek and Roman Empires, and into modern times with the East and the West. The rise and fall of the Third Reich saw how fast a nation can rise and fall as Nazi Germany nearly conquered the world through its *blitzkrieg* lightning attacks and victories in Europe and North Africa. They might have succeeded had it not been for the courage of the Allies and the purposes of God. Again, at the turn of the decade into the 1990's, we observed what at close range had to be one of the most incredible turn of events in contemporary history. The great "evil empire" (so-called by former President Ronald Reagan) began to unravel and dissolve right before our eyes. Who would have expected that communism, which had appeared on the world stage a scant 70 years earlier, would fall so quickly? The militant Marxism, which had intimidated a world with its godless rule based on military might, was suddenly impotent. The multi-headed hydra monster headquartered in Moscow with tentacles reaching around the world was mortally wounded. Afghanistan became their Vietnam—draining resources, manpower, and finances in a war that in the end seemed pointless. This powerful ideology failed because of one simple fact: It did not work!

Original Sin

Bible students could have predicted communism's failure based on original sin. Since Adam's sin and fall from grace in the garden of Eden, every man and woman has been born with a natural tendency toward sin. Selfishness is the most obvious attribute of sin, just as selflessness is an attribute of righteousness. Everyone naturally takes care of "number one." Those who try to refute this fact need only to look into a baby's crib where two babies are placed with only one rattle. What ensues could possibly be compared with World War III on a baby scale. It has often been pointed out that selfishness is automatic, whereas laying down one's self will is a learned trait, and a hard-earned one at that. Thus, communism was destined to fail because it was based on a philosophy that presumed the good will of men—that they would all work very hard and productively for the common good. However, the nature of man was proven once again: lust for money, power, domination, and violence was compounded by laziness, envy, and rebellion. In short, man is sinful.

Communal sharing is an ideal that is clearly unreachable for unregenerate men and women. In fact, if we are honest, even born-again and Spirit-filled Christians have difficulty dealing with the "old nature." "In a moment, in the twinkling of an eye, at the last trumpet. For the trumpet will sound, and the dead will be raised incorruptible, and we shall be changed. For this corruptible must put on incorruption, and this mortal must put on immortality" (1 Cor. 15:52-53). In other words, we are still corruptible until Jesus returns. We would prefer that God wave a magic wand and make us perfect, but He prefers that we go through a process similar to that of His Son Jesus: "Though He was a Son, yet He learned obedience by the things which He suffered" (Heb. 5:8). We are learning to follow the Lord His way.

The Fall of Democracy

Before we Americans start getting any egotistical ideas, we also need to consider democracy. The history of the durability of democracies is not much better.

> More than 200 years ago, while the original 13 colonies were still part of Great Britain, Professor Alexander Tyler wrote of the Athenian republic, which had fallen 2000 years earlier: "A democracy cannot exist as a permanent form of government. It can only exist until the voters discover that they can vote themselves a largesse from the [public] treasury. From that moment on, the majority will always vote for the candidates promising the most benefits from the public treasury, with the result that a democracy always collapses over loose fiscal policy and is always followed by a dictatorship. The average age of the world's greatest civilizations has been 200 years. These nations have progressed through this sequence: From BONDAGE

to SPIRITUAL FAITH; from SPIRITUAL FAITH to GREAT COURAGE; from GREAT COURAGE to ABUNDANCE; from ABUNDANCE to SELFISHNESS; from SELFISHNESS to COMPLACENCY; from COMPLACENCY to APATHY; from APATHY to DEPENDENCY; from DEPENDENCY back again into BONDAGE."(1)

What stage of transition do you think the United States is in now? Perhaps the World Wars showed our great courage. Were the 1950's our abundance, followed by the selfish "Me Generation" of the 1960's? Have the 1970's and 1980's really been the transition from complacency to apathy? Are things moving that fast? Maybe not, but if this amazing definition of the downfall of democracy fits our situation then the stage of dependency is next for the 1990's. That scenario is not as unthinkable as it once was; the nation that fed the world could be bankrupt and in bondage before the year 2000!

The United States now measures its national debt at more than three *trillion* dollars. Estimates suggest that the debt of the private business community equals that amount. The third area of debt is more telling than the first two: personal consumer debt is also said to be three trillion dollars! All of this debt points to an extremely vulnerable economy in this country. If the two superpowers of the modern world are on the brink of economic ruin, what or who will fill the vacuum created by such a devastating collapse? The answer could be Islam, a unified European Economic Community, New Age humanism, or any combination of these powers or other unforeseen developments. The one thing we do know is the Bible predicts that Israel and the Middle East will be right in the thick of things.

Democratic Peace

Some would like to believe that democracy will win the world and the nations will dwell in peace. In the 1989 student demonstration in China, a model of the Statue of Liberty was raised in Tianamen Square and they called it "the goddess of liberty." You can be sure that the God of the Bible will have no other gods before Him, including this goddess! No, democracy will not save the human race. American democracy has worked partially because the founding fathers believed the Bible and structured our government with the presupposition of original sin. They devised a system of checks and balances with three branches of government that has made it much more difficult for a despot to gain control. However, in the time of an economic collapse, people could be so desperate that they would welcome a powerful leader who would promise prosperity in return for total authority. This scenario was demonstrated in Russia where Boris Yeltsin, in December of 1993, asked for and received a vote of confidence for his presidency and for increased powers for his office. Is this scenario going to happen in America? Or is it just a nightmare? I hope so. Will it ever happen? I hope not, but even if it does, my faith is not in any human government, but in the God of Heaven who has everything under control.

We do not know all that will unfold in the months and years ahead, but I strongly believe that Israel is a key player in whatever is to come.

Behold, I will make Jerusalem a cup of drunkenness [literally, "reeling"] *to all the surrounding peoples, when they lay siege against Judah and Jerusalem. And it shall happen in that day that I will make Jerusalem a very heavy stone for all peoples; all who would heave it away will surely be cut in pieces, though all the nations of the earth are gathered against it* (Zechariah 12:2-3).

Again, these verses must refer to a future time because of the phrase "all the nations of the earth." Here also is the promise of their salvation in verse 10: "And I will pour on the house of David and on the inhabitants of Jerusalem the Spirit of grace and supplication; then they will look on Me whom they have pierced. Yes, they will mourn for Him as one mourns for his only son, and grieve for Him as one grieves for a firstborn." This mention of "Me whom they have pierced" dates this prophecy to some future time not only after the time of Zechariah but sometime after the death of Jesus. The prophecy continues:

"In that day a fountain shall be opened for the house of David and for the inhabitants of Jerusalem, for sin and for uncleanness. It shall be in that day," says the Lord of hosts, *"that I will cut off the names of the idols from the land, and they shall no longer be remembered. I will also cause the prophets and the unclean spirit to depart from the land"* (Zechariah 13:1-2).

What a glorious time of repentance and forgiveness waits for God's covenant nation! There is no doubt that Israel fell, but there is equally no doubt in the Scriptures of her restoration and salvation in the end. We have seen the historical overview of Israel, but to find out how we get from history to fulfillment, we should look at what is happening today.

GOD IS FAITHFUL!

Chapter 9

The Contemporary Jewish Problem

There is a contemporary reason for us to consider Israel. Contrary to the idea of a "Jewish problem" as viewed by Adolph Hitler, which was based on a perverse form of extreme racism, there is a real theological question. A prophecy in Romans 11 says that Israel will be saved. How will her salvation be perceived by the Christian community? When this fulfillment continues to unfold, there will be much consternation among Christians around the world. There are two reasons this will bother them. First, most Christians are not expecting it to literally happen. Second, it will happen in a way they do not like. A real key to this issue is found in Acts 15, which we will examine in order. Then we will discuss the actual process of salvation from a Jewish perspective.

Can Israel Really Be Saved?

Israel's salvation is clearly prophesied in Romans 11:25-27:

For I do not desire, brethren, that you should be ignorant of this mystery, lest you should be wise in your own opinion, that blindness in part has happened to Israel until the fullness of the Gentiles has come in. And so all Israel will be saved, as it is written: "The Deliverer will come out of Zion, and He will turn away ungodliness from Jacob; for this is My covenant with them, when I take away their sins."

Paul states his revelation and then quotes Isaiah 59:20 as his authority. The key phrases are "turn away ungodliness *from Jacob*...take away their sins." The reference to Jacob indicates that the physical descendants of Israel are the topic here, not spiritual Israel. God certainly intends to save Israel for His name's sake, whether we like it or not. If there is a conflict between our theology and God's actual will, guess who has to change?

Allow me to only lightly deal with the question of "all" Israel being saved by a simple comment: This is a parallel idea to the New Testament concept that "all" the elect will be saved. In other words, every single person who is ever destined to choose salvation will, in fact, be saved at some certain point in history. At such time the total actually saved will be viewed as the only true Church or Israel. So a great turning to Jesus as the Messiah will occur in the near future among the Jews, which will bring in all the rest of the eternal Israel of God. Those who refuse Him will be lost, exactly as it is with the rest of us. I am not saying there is another salvation for Israel; the Jews must come through Jesus. That is a non-negotiable fact for them, whether they like it or not. The miracle is that they will accept Jesus!

Christian Attitudes

The main question is much more practical. What will be the general reaction of Christians as this phenomenal process is taking place? There will be various attitudes including confusion, disagreement, anger, indignation and resentment. Such reactions will occur because of widespread ignorance of a simple bit of biblical wisdom that should be properly applied to this terminal time period. I believe a situation recorded in the Book of Acts will *reoccur*, but in the opposite way. The reason for this reversal is the reversal of the statistics. In the early first century Church, virtually all who believed in Jesus as the Messiah were Jews. Jesus was a Jew not only by birth, but also by culture. Peter, James, John, Paul, and just about every other early leader and believer were all Jews! It was an amazing and nearly unbelievable concept to those Jewish apostles when God began to reveal that Gentiles could also be saved! Today, just the opposite is true, statistically. Almost all believers are Gentile. Why is this significant? Before God began restoring Israel, it was not a problem. When Jews were saved, which was rare, they usually left their Jewish cultural identity behind to join the church. This suited the rest of us just fine. In fact, it tended to vindicate some of our own unbiblical church traditions and worse, it confirmed our independent arrogance with regard to Israel. The Church has become so strong and so completely "Gentile-ized" that we have temporarily lost the awareness of our critically important roots in Judaism.

We have developed a whole set of traditional Christian feasts and celebrations such as Lent, Maundy Thursday, Good Friday, Easter, and Christmas. In our desire and enthusiasm to build a tradition around Jesus, we have possibly overstepped our bounds. Where is it written in the Bible that we should celebrate these occasions as "holy feasts"? Personally, I especially enjoy celebrating Christmas, even though its roots are in Roman Catholic tradition. Yet there are biblical feasts of the Lord that we have forgotten. The last great feast that has yet to have a New Testament fulfillment is the Feast of Tabernacles, which is the ingathering of the harvest. We are getting excited now to realize that the great fulfillment of that feast is to take place in these endtimes. All over the world people are being saved as the gospel is taken to the ends of the earth. Rejecting the Old Testament as passé is a big mistake. The entire Bible is still relevant. I am not necessarily saying we should not observe our Christian holidays; I am saying that, we should watch our attitudes in judging Jews who observe the biblical feasts.

Messianic Judaism

There is a new part to this problem. God is saving Israel and these new Jewish believers are not all joining our neighborhood churches. This has been a shock for many of us. But there is a new move of God in the earth called Messianic Judaism. This movement is rising rapidly on the world scene and is causing questions from both sides. Christians don't know what to think and Jews are threatened by it. My friend, Haim Levi (President of the Messianic Jewish Alliance of America), estimates that there are currently a half-million Messianic Jews worldwide! He also reports that Messianic Jewish Conferences now circle the entire globe, from the United States to Argentina, Mexico, South Africa, Australia, Israel, and now to Russia. A 1993 conference in St. Petersburg, Russia, drew some 3,000 Jews! In Orlando, Florida, the annual conference gathers 1,000 Jews from the Southeast U.S.A. and Latin America. The

The Contemporary Jewish Problem

Jerusalem Post, an Israeli English-language newspaper, has referred to Messianic Judaism as the "fourth stream" of Judaism, after the Orthodox, Conservative, and Reform. It is also true that many secular Jews do not identify with any of the four.

As with everything else God is doing, there is also a satanic counterfeit for Messianic Judaism. It rises periodically to name one of their own as the messiah. It is getting so you can't tell the messiahs without a scorecard. That is why we need to look to the Bible for every detail of the facts confirming the true Messiah, Jesus. I must admit that it is fun to see God confusing all the religious folks with the truth. This confusion is not just among the Jews though, for many Christians don't understand what is going on either. But they do know that they do not like it; it disturbs the status quo.

Jews are being genuinely saved and are starting their own congregations! We Christians with our hundreds of denominations, many of which started with splits and fights, actually have the audacity to be indignant toward this "upstart" Messianic movement! Yet they at least have a legitimate case. They want to worship on the Sabbath day and continue to observe the biblical feasts. In addition, they actually want to keep their cultural traditions! What nerve! Why are we so generous with pagans who get saved by allowing—and in fact encouraging them—to preserve their distinctive cultural heritage, as long as it does not contradict the biblical standards? Couldn't we give the Messianic Jewish believers as much grace? But when Jews get saved, we demand that they renounce their ancient God-given culture and traditions and in effect become "Gentile-ized." This is a big mistake. It is quite a paradox. There is a warning given to Gentiles by the apostle Paul:

Do not boast against the branches. But if you do boast, remember that you do not support the root, but the root supports you. You will say then, "Branches were broken off that I might be grafted in." Well said. Because of unbelief they were broken off, and you stand by faith. Do not be haughty, but fear. For if God did not spare the natural branches, He may not spare you either (Romans 11:18-21).

Acts 15

This brings us to the council at Jerusalem. We need to look at this critical historical consultation that occurred in the very beginning of the Christian Church. This meeting convened in Jerusalem at the request of the apostles in that city because the spread of the gospel to Gentiles was giving rise to new questions. There was among the believers a strong faction who were known as Judaizers. They insisted that all the new Gentile converts to Jesus also adopt the cultural heritage and religious traditions of the Jews. On the other hand, Paul and Barnabas did not believe it was necessary. Thus, the Jerusalem conference made an historic decision that paved the way for the millions of Gentile believers through the centuries. They were called Nazarenes or followers of the Way until Antioch, where they were first called Christians or "little annointed ones" because they had the same annointing as Jesus.

After much prayer and articulate testimony from each leader, James stood and summarized the conclusions and suggested that a letter be written to the Gentile believers to inform them of the decision, a portion of which is quoted here:

Since we have heard that some who went out from us have troubled you with words, unsettling your souls,

> *saying, "You must be circumcised and keep the law"—to whom we gave no such commandment—it seemed good to us, being assembled with one accord, to send chosen men to you with our beloved Barnabas and Paul, men who have risked their lives for the name of our Lord Jesus Christ. We have therefore sent Judas and Silas, who will also report the same things by word of mouth. For it seemed good to the Holy Spirit, and to us, to lay upon you no greater burden than these necessary things: that you abstain from things offered to idols, from blood, from things strangled, and from sexual immorality. If you keep yourselves from these, you will do well. Farewell* (Acts 15:24-29).

They did not need to be circumcised; it was enough that they believed in Jesus.

Today's Wisdom

Therefore, I would like to suggest we apply the same wisdom today to the Body of Christ that is now comprised mostly of Gentiles. Jews who are being saved should not be asked to do any more than Gentiles were 2,000 years ago. It is enough that they receive Jesus and believe in Him. They do not have to become "culturally circumcised" into our Gentile traditions. Of course, they must believe the Bible and abstain from any kind of idols, ancient or modern, just as we must. But the wisdom of Acts 15 stands today as does the witness of the Holy Spirit. Surely we can say to them, "Welcome, brethren, it is enough that you believe in Jesus!"

As God removes the veil from their eyes and they finally see Jesus, let us rejoice and assist them in every way possible. God forbid that we should be a hindrance to them, making their seeing more difficult. Praise God that there are now thousands of Messianic believers in hundreds of congregations around the world, including Israel! Pray for unity in Jesus and their example or witness before their own brethren.

GOD IS FAITHFUL!

Chapter 10

The Paradox of Jewish Salavation

The salvation of modern Jews is a paradox for many Christians, but it is even more so from the perspective of the Jew. He asks himself, "How can a man, who believes in the God who allows no other gods before Him, *convert* to worshiping the 'Christian' Gods of Father, Son, and Holy Spirit?" If you can understand this dilemma of the modern Jew, then read on, for there are biblical answers to his questions.

Blasphemy!

The fact that Christians claim to be monotheists seems like a contradiction to most Jews. They hear us call Jesus the Son of God. They know that our creeds and the New Testament declare His Deity! They can read for themselves His own claims as He spoke to a group of rebellious Jews:

"Your father Abraham rejoiced to see My day, and he saw it and was glad." Then the Jews said to Him, *"You*

are not yet fifty years old, and have You seen Abraham?" Jesus said to them, "Most assuredly, I say to you, before Abraham was, I AM" (John 8:56-58).

The reaction of those to whom Jesus was speaking was to take up stones to stone Him to death! The fact that they were unsuccessful does not detract from their intent. Why did they want to kill Him? They considered His words blasphemous. Not only did He claim to be alive before Abraham, but He used the exact same verb form "I AM," that God used in His call and instructions to Moses at the burning bush. Moses had asked God an amazing question about His name:

... "Indeed, when I come to the children of Israel and say to them, 'The God of your fathers has sent me to you,' and they say to me, 'What is His name?' what shall I say to them?" And God said to Moses, "I AM WHO I AM." And He said, "Thus you shall say to the children of Israel, 'I AM has sent me to you' " (Exodus 3:13-14).

On many other occasions in the New Testament, Jesus was accused of blasphemy. There is no doubt that He claimed to be the Son of God in the sense of Deity. There is no doubt that those who heard Him took it that way and would have killed Him on several occasions before finally succeeding with the help of the Romans. There is no doubt that the apostle Paul held the same view:

Let this mind be in you which was also in Christ Jesus, who, being in the form of God, did not consider it robbery to be equal with God, but made Himself of no reputation, taking the form of a bondservant, and coming in the likeness of men. And being found in appearance as a man, He humbled Himself and became obedient to the point of death, even the death of the cross (Philippians 2:5-8).

In other words, Jesus' claims were clear. There were then, and are now, only two choices: He was either a liar or He is the Son of God!

No Other Gods

The Ten Commandments given to Israel by God through Moses have become the foundational standard of civil law for most of Western civilization through the centuries. They stand intact today, in spite of the fact that they are no longer allowed in American public schools. Even if they are ignored by our sinful and permissive generation (reduced to the "Ten Suggestions"), they still stand as God's standard. To observant Jews, there is no greater commandment than the first: "You shall have no other gods before Me" (Ex. 20:3). This specifically included carved images and any likeness of *anything* in heaven or earth. With these rather clear parameters, it is no wonder they have trouble with Christianity and all our pictures, statues, and even the tiny "dashboard Jesus"! It is my humble opinion that we who have participated in these things have much to be ashamed of in Christendom and more than a little explaining to do when we face the Lord in the Day of Judgment.

What advantage then has the Jew, or what is the profit of circumcision? Much in every way! Chiefly because to them were committed the oracles of God. For what if some did not believe? Will their unbelief make the faithfulness of God without effect? Certainly not! Indeed, let God be true but every man a liar... (Romans 3:1-4).

Are Jews Pagan?

Do Jews worship gods made with men's hands? Do you see the problem from their perspective? Certainly there are many pagan Jews who are atheists, Marxists, humanists, or occultists. These Jews are clearly unbelievers in every sense of the word. But what about those Jews who believe in the God of Abraham, Isaac, and Jacob? Is He not the only true God? Are these particular Jews pagan? Must they *forsake* their God to accept a "Christian God," as though He were not one and the same? This is *not* a moot point. It is the crux of the matter. Many Christians, in their zeal to save Jews, end up confusing the issue. A Jew may love God and desire to know Him and serve Him. Our opportunity is to tell about the Messiah who died to save him in fulfillment of all the promises of the God of Abraham, Isaac, and Jacob! With pagans, we start with the need to renounce all other gods. But with Jews who believe in God, we have a head start. They do not need to renounce their God because they are worshiping the right God already! They simply need to learn about and receive His Son Jesus, the Jewish Messiah.

God Is One!

There is a deeper theological problem for the sincerely seeking Jew. For centuries they have repeated what is known as the "Shema Yisrael," which is a Bible verse: "Hear, O Israel: The Lord our God, the Lord is one!" (Deut. 6:4) This verse has had a powerful effect on the Jewish people for millennia, but in relatively recent centuries it has taken on meaning that is almost bigger than life. A very famous Hebrew rabbi of the fifteenth century named Maimonides made a profound contribution to Jewish tradition. As a matter of fact, he was quite instrumental in the advance of Kabalism, which is a kind of Jewish mysticism considered by Christians to be occult. His most profound effect on history was over a very simple point regarding the Shema. He noticed that the Hebrew word translated as *one* in that verse was troubling to his personal concept of God. Instead of changing his belief though, he changed the word. He did not, of course, try to change it in the Torah, the actual Scripture text, because that was strictly forbidden. He did, however, use it in his teaching that is recorded in the Talmud, the rabbinical biblical commentaries.

Why all this fuss about a little word? It actually is a critical point. The Hebrew word in the Hebrew Bible text is *echad*. The word Mamonides substituted in his teaching was the Hebrew word *yachid*. The subtle difference, in this apparently small adjustment of emphasis, has created one of the greatest blockages to Jewish salvation that exists today. *Yachid* means "one," but in an indivisible singular sense that when used in the Shema, makes God singular and absolutely indivisible. This certainly is the Jewish concept of God that prevails today. However, the word *echad* is the actual word for *one* in the original text and carries a profoundly different meaning. It means "one" also, but in the sense of a *plural* unity. This point is critical in understanding how Jesus and the Holy Spirit fit into our understanding of God.

We can easily confirm this point by checking how *echad* is used in other Bible texts. In an earlier chapter we studied Ezekiel 37:17 regarding the reuniting of the kingdom of Israel and the kingdom of Judah using two sticks: "Then join them one to another for yourself into *one* stick, and they will become *one* in your hand." Here two kingdoms of people become one, which indicates a spiritual and political unity made up of many people. The phrases "one people" or "one nation" are used numerous times in the Hebrew Scriptures. Yet there is an even more convincing text: "Therefore a man shall leave his father and mother and be joined to his wife, and they shall become *one* flesh" (Gen. 2:24). This is the same word, *echad*, that is used in the Shema: "The Lord is one!" In other words, there is *one* God in a plural sense of unity who has revealed Himself as Father, Son, and Holy Spirit!

This discovery meets the test of interpreting Scripture by Scripture, which is also seen in another, better-known example: "In the beginning God created the heavens and the earth" (Gen. 1:1). In the first verse of the Bible, the word translated *God* is the Hebrew word *Elohim*, which has a *plural* ending! This is used throughout Genesis 1 and, in fact, the entire Old Testament. The idea of a plurality within God is further indicated with this verse: "Then God said, 'Let *Us* make man in *Our* image, according to *Our* likeness…' " (Gen. 1:26). Again, plural words are used in reference to God. The reason it is so hard for people to accept this idea of one God who is plural in manifestation, is our proven human disunity. We can't seem to get along with anybody else. Even marriage, which God intended as a prime example of unity, has come under such attack that some people do not know even one couple who are a bona fide model of unity. Yet, our human failure does not invalidate God's revelation. "Two shall be one" is still God's purpose and there are still believing couples who are enjoying such unity!

We quoted a passage earlier in this chapter from Philippians 2 that described Jesus' emptying Himself of His Deity to submit to the Father's will in the death on the cross. We know this was necessary so His blood could be the ultimate payment for sin. John the Baptist revealed Him as "the Lamb of God who takes away the sin of the world" (Jn. 1:29). Jesus became the Lamb of atonement, not to cover sin for another year according to the law, but to *take away* the sins of the world according to mercy and grace.

Therefore God also has highly exalted Him and given Him the name which is above every name, that at the name of Jesus every knee should bow, of those in heaven, and of those on earth, and of those under the earth, and that every tongue should confess that Jesus Christ is Lord, to the glory of God the Father (Philippians 2:9-11).

Notice that the glory ultimately goes to the Father. Even though Jesus is equal with God, there is still a placement within this order. This same concept is also taught for marriages: equal in value, but different in function. Husband and wife have equal value, but a functional hierarchy is necessary for practical operations on a day-to-day basis.

Jesus is honored further in another passage:

Giving thanks to the Father who has qualified us to be partakers of the inheritance of the saints in the light. He has delivered us from the power of darkness and conveyed us into the kingdom of the Son of His love, in whom we have redemption through His blood, the forgiveness of sins. He is the image of the invisible God, the firstborn over all creation, For by Him all things were created that are in heaven and that are on earth, visible and invisible, whether thrones or dominions or principalities or powers. All things were created through Him and for Him. And He is before all things, and in Him all things consist. And He is the head of the body, the church, who is the beginning, the firstborn from the dead, that in all things He may have the preeminence (Colossians 1:12-18).

Prophesy to the Land

The Jewish people are going to see Jesus in scriptural light in these last days and receive Him as their Messiah and Lord. "Oh, that the salvation of Israel would come out of Zion! When the Lord brings back the captivity of His people, let Jacob rejoice and Israel be glad" (Ps. 14:7). When God does this supernatural work, what will be your reaction? What a thrilling day to be alive as witnesses to these things!

GOD IS FAITHFUL!

Chapter 11

God's Faithful Covenant

The land and the people of Israel indeed have a unique relationship with God. It is true that He is Lord of all, but one of His titles that is used most often is "the God of Abraham, Isaac, and Jacob." Until the revelation of Jesus, we are given no personal "first" name of God. The Almighty is known as the God of these three men! He is revealed through their personal names. This is not a superfluous mentioning for the promised seed is through this specific lineage:

Nor are they all children because they are the seed of Abraham; but, "In Isaac your seed shall be called." That is, those who are the children of the flesh, these are not the children of God; but the children of the promise are counted as the seed. For this is the word of promise: "At this time I will come and Sarah shall have a son." And not only this, but when Rebecca also had conceived by one man, even by our father Isaac (for the children not yet being born, nor having done any good or evil, that the purpose of God according to election might stand, not of works but of Him who calls), it was said to her, "The older shall serve the younger." As it is written, "Jacob I have loved, but Esau I have hated" (Romans 9:7-13).

The promised Messiah would come through Jacob by God's sovereign choice. We may not like it, but it stands. It is perplexing for us to grasp the clear fact of the statement that God chose Jacob and rejected Esau *before* either of them did *anything* to influence His choice!

The Mercy of God

It is this mercy aspect of God's sovereignty that is the *premise behind the promise* of salvation. God is God. We are saved entirely by His merciful choice to save us—Jew or Gentile. We do not sit in judgment of Him, but He will judge us. We glean the promises of Scripture to find where we fit in. We are given a choice; we can accept our places in His plan or reject it. The most frightening fact I know about God is that He actually will allow us to refuse Him. But by the same token, if we accept His merciful offer, we can live with Him forever! Our only option is to accept the offer or reject it. We cannot choose our natural family or our national heritage, we are born into it. We either accept our parents or reject them, but we do not choose new birth parents. There is therefore a promise through Abraham, Isaac, and Jacob that stands by God's will and not by the choice of any man, and it is God who will keep His faithful promises to their seed.

The Original Promise

Let's take a look now at the original covenant that God gave to Abraham while his name was still Abram :

Now the Lord said to Abram: "Get out of your country, from your family and from your father's house, to a land that I will show you. I will make you a great nation; I will bless you and make your name great; and you shall be a blessing. I will bless those who bless you, and I will curse him who curses you; And in you all the families of the earth shall be blessed" (Genesis 12:1-3).

God's blessing to the earth is fulfilled in the Messiah Jesus who is the literal seed of Abraham and who provided eternal life to all who believe in Him of all nations, races, and tribes of the earth. After Abram was too old to have any children he asked God about it, and God again spoke His covenant to Abram:

And behold, the word of the Lord came to him, saying, "This one shall not be your heir, but one who will come from your own body shall be your heir." Then He brought him outside and said, "Look now toward heaven, and count the stars if you are able to number them." And He said to him, "So shall your descendants be." And he believed in the Lord, and He accounted it to him for righteousness. Then He said to him, "I am the Lord, who brought you out of Ur of the Chaldeans, to give you this land to inherit it" (Genesis 15:4-7).

This event took place before Abraham was circumcised. (This has a major point in Romans 11 which we will consider in due course.) Abram believed God, and he was credited with righteousness not for *doing*, but for *believing*. Even in Genesis he was not saved by the law, but by the grace and mercy of God.

Israel's Borders

People often ask me what the biblical borders of Israel were that define the land given to Abram. The answer is stated clearly later in the passage we have just been reading: "On the same day the Lord made a covenant with Abram, saying: 'To your descendants I have given this land, from the river of Egypt to the great river, the River Euphrates' " (Gen. 15:18). This area includes present day Israel and also parts of Egypt, Jordan, Syria, and Lebanon. How Israel obtains that extra land is in God's hands. My wife Doreen and I began publishing *Israel NewsCard* every other week in January 1990, and I made the comment in one issue that the whole world is watching the West Bank (of the Jordan River) but we should actually be watching the East Bank. People devise their own plans, but in the end it will be God's Word that is accomplished.

> *He will set up a banner for the nations, and will assemble the outcasts of Israel, and gather together the dispersed of Judah from the four corners of the earth. Also the envy of Ephraim shall depart, and the adversaries of Judah shall be cut off; Ephraim shall not envy Judah, and Judah shall not harass Ephraim. But they shall fly down upon the shoulder of the Philistines toward the west; together they shall plunder the people of the East; they shall lay their hand on Edom and Moab; and the people of Ammon shall obey them* (Isaiah 11:12-14).

The areas mentioned are again quite clear. The "shoulder of the Philistines" must refer to the West Bank and Gaza area, which has been through another uprising of today's Palestinians (which is from the same Hebrew word as Philistines, as explained earlier). Evidently this conflict will be resolved with Israel possessing the land in question. Also, Isaiah prophesies that Israel will defeat "the people of the East... Edom...Moab...Ammon"—all of which are in modern day Jordan. Perhaps you now see why we must watch the East Bank.

Land Covenant

The theme of this book came from Ezekiel 36, as we discussed in Chapter 1. The premise of this book is the faithfulness of God as exemplified first by His character, His own unchangeable nature. God does not *act* faithful—He *is* faithful! We saw that He gave an oath to a land and a people that He intends to keep. The second part of this book has dealt with the promises in the Word of God where God recorded for all posterity the exact facts of His purpose in the earth. The last section deals with His faithful fulfillment of these promises. But before we move on we should look at more of the specific promises to the land and to Abraham, Isaac, and Jacob.

The ownership of the Holy Land resides with God: "The earth is the Lord's, and all its fullness" (Ps. 24:1a). He may give it to whomever He chooses. "And He has made from one blood every nation of men to dwell on all the face of the earth, and has determined their preappointed times and the boundaries of their dwellings, so that they should seek the Lord..." (Acts 17:26-27). He not only sets their borders, He also sets the limits and the extent of the time they are permitted to live there!

> *For behold, in those days and at that time, when I bring back the captives of Judah and Jerusalem, I will also gather all nations, and bring them down to the Valley of Jehoshaphat; and I will enter into judgment with them **there** on account of My people, My heritage Israel, whom they have scattered among the nations; they have also divided up **My land*** (Joel 3:1-2).

Prophesy to the Land

Here again is the unmistakable reference to the scattering of the Diaspora. This is a literal promise of the living God set within clear parameters of time and geography. This is not some nebulous symbolic suggestion; it is a warning of God's precise plan to judge the nations directly in proportion to *how* they treated God's land and His people. He even indicts them for dividing His land. Could there be a clearer verse that describes the actions of the United Nation's continually sitting in judgment of Israel? They keep partitioning the land and demanding that the Israelis give more of it back to the Arabs. They are playing God—but He owns the land and He will set the boundaries!

This is even more clearly spoken to Abraham at the time when God changed his name from Abram, "exalted father," to "father of a multitude."

> *And I will establish My covenant between Me and you and your descendants after you in their generations, for an **everlasting** covenant, to be God to you and your descendants after you. Also I give to you and your descendants after you the **land** in which you are a stranger, all the **land** of Canaan, as an **everlasting** possession; and I will be their God* (Genesis 17:7-8).

This not only states who will have the land—it also declares that they will know God.

We also maintained earlier in this chapter that the Messianic promises were *not to all* of Abraham's offspring, which includes the descendants of Ishmael and Esau who were children of the flesh, or man's attempts. The covenant was limited to Isaac and Jacob. Even in Jesus, when the whole world may come to Him, the Messianic covenant is through the seed of Abraham, Isaac, and Jacob as the way we are joined into the root of Israel. Thus the land covenant and blessing was continued to Isaac:

*Dwell in this land, and I will be with you and bless you; for to you and your descendants I give all these **lands**, and I will perform the oath which I swore to Abraham your father. And I will make your descendants multiply as the stars of heaven; I will give to your descendants all these **lands**; and in your seed all the nations of the earth shall be blessed* (Genesis 26:3-4).

And finally, the promise is continued also to Jacob:

*And God said to him, "Your name is Jacob; your name shall not be called Jacob anymore, but Israel shall be your name." So He called his name Israel. Also God said to him: "I am God Almighty. Be fruitful and multiply; a nation and a company of nations shall proceed from you, and kings shall come from your body. The **land** which I gave Abraham and Isaac I give to you; and to your descendants after you I give this **land**"* (Genesis 35:10-12).

Is there any room for doubt about God's intentions?

Five-Fold Emphasis

There is a clear description of Psalm 105:8-11 in an excellent book by Derek Prince, which I quote here:

...the psalmist goes on to proclaim the specific judgments, or determinations, of God concerning the land of Canaan: "He remembers his covenant forever, the word he commanded, for a thousand generations, the covenant he made with Abraham, the oath he swore to Isaac. He confirmed it to Jacob as a decree, to Israel as an everlasting covenant: 'To you I will give the land of Canaan as the portion you will inherit.' " The psalmist emphasizes two important points. First, he leaves no doubt as to the line of descent through which the promise of the land is given. It is from Abraham, to Isaac, to Jacob, to Israel. Second, the psalmist uses every conceivable scriptural term to establish the sacred, unchanging nature of God's commitment to Abraham and his descendants. He speaks of God's own "covenant," and of "the word he commanded," and of "the oath he swore." Then he speaks of "a decree" and finally of "an everlasting covenant." What a powerful list of words denoting God's unchanging commitment: covenant, word, command, oath, decree and, finally, everlasting covenant! I know of no other passage where Scripture speaks with greater or more sustained emphasis than this. And all this emphasis centers around one issue: the ownership of the land of Canaan.(1)

This reference to a thousand generations is amazing. Even if you only figured 40 years per generation, it would be 40,000 years! I don't think God is done with Israel just yet.

Never Uprooted Again

Allow me to end this chapter with another quotation from Derek Prince:

When God promises to bring Israel back to the land at the close of the age, He still calls it "your own land." In God's sight, the ownership of the land has never changed and never will. He gave it to Abraham and his descendants by an everlasting covenant. Finally, let us turn again briefly to Amos. "I will plant Israel in their own land, never again to be uprooted from the land I have given them, says the Lord your God" (Amos 9:15). Here again, God is speaking of Israel's end-time restoration in "their own land." Furthermore, He promises that they will never again be uprooted. This promise, given nearly 3,000 years ago, is neither affected nor modified by the growing might of the Arab nations today, nor by their determination to destroy Israel. On the contrary, the current multiplication of problems and the violent opposition to Israel shows us why God, in His foresight, took such pains to emphasize Israel's inalienable right to the land.(2)

We stand in awe of the sovereign and faithful God who will keep every promise in His Word. I told many people as I wrote this book that it is not about Israel; it is about the faithfulness of God. Israel is His banner or His illustration to reveal His faithful character, His faithful word, and His faithful fulfillment.

GOD IS FAITHFUL!

Part III

The Precision: The Faithfulness of God's Fulfillment

Chapter 12

Homogenous History

We looked at the biblical outline of history in Chapter 7, but now we will look at history from another perspective. God could have had a succession of kingdoms like man did, as well as a series of plans as discussed in Chapter 3, but He did not do things in that way. He has had one single purpose from the beginning and all of history revolves around His plan like the planets orbit the sun. The beauty of this perspective is how everything precisely fits into His plan. This third part looks at the *precision* of God's faithfulness to fulfill His plan.

Most Christians are aware of the intricate patchwork of prophecies regarding the coming of the Messiah, each fulfilled exactly by Jesus, and how there are plenty more that point to His second coming. It is tempting to think that God sort of "let things roll" and adapted His plan as the events unfolded. But God is not at the mercy of events; He ordains the events of time to further His own original purpose. *He does not change plans to fit the circumstances; He changes circumstances to fit His plan!*

Prophesy to the Land

Messianic prophecies were confusing to religious leaders before Jesus' birth. There were arguments about where the Messiah would come from. Some said Bethlehem, some said Galilee, and some even said Egypt. The amazing fulfillment had Him born in Bethlehem, flee to Egypt, and then be raised in Nazareth! It was all true and it made sense after it happened. The same is true for the prophecies of the restoration of Israel. They are somewhat confusing before they happen, but make sense once they are fulfilled. For example, there are Scriptures that talk about Israel being rejected for her spiritual adultery, and other verses say God will have mercy and restore her in the end. Some argue about which of these is true, but *both* are true. Israel is to be *both* rejected *and* restored!

There is a natural tendency in the pride of man to look at his own day and think that all history issues from him. Any nation that ever became much of anything thought it was everything. During the development of the present superpowers, it was possible to live in the United States or the U.S.S.R. and think either was it. In the West, especially in England and the United States, there were those who believed something called British Israelism. After the rise of the British Empire, and lacking evidence at that time in history of a literal restoration of physical Israel, it was quite easy to spiritualize the prophecies toward Great Britain. It was believed in many quarters that England and her commonwealth of nations were the Israel of the Bible restored. The unfortunate side of this belief was that its reinforcement of the sinful side of our nature to believe in a racial preference of God. Many people sincerely believed (and some still do) that the White Anglo-Saxon people were the real Israel. Thankfully, this deceptive prejudice is now exposed by the unfolding of recent prophetic events. It is hard to retain a subjective view in light of the objective facts of history. There is a physical Israel being restored complete with religion, government, culture, language, and most importantly, a land and a people.

This is where the precision is revealed. Israel is not a new place carved out of Brazil or somewhere else. It is located exactly where ancient Israel was given to the forefathers. The idea that this could have come about by the cunning of men instead of the divine plan, strains the credibility of those insisting such. I could understand those who held that view before the rebirth of Israel in 1948, or even before the Six Day War of 1967, but it is nothing short of stubbornness to hold on to a view that has been smashed by the actual fulfillments of history.

For years now, hardly a day goes by that you can't pick up a newspaper from any city and find a significant story about Israel or Egypt or one of the other Bible nations. This is a very recent phenomena—the attention of the world is coming back to the Middle East, right on schedule for the end of the age. This is not a symbolic emphasis; it is literal and it is actually happening. Arab oil interests, wars, earthquakes, terrorism, hostage-taking, debates in the United Nations, and territorial disputes are happening all over the area of biblical geography. Within Israel we see the desert blossoming like a rose, ancient biblical cities being rebuilt and inhabited, the people multiplying like a flock, and signs of people turning to Jesus as the Messiah of Israel!

The dominant development outside Israel is the rise of Islamic Fundamentalism. This allows for the reappearance of the ancient enemies of Israel from the Bible: the descendants of

Ishmael, Esau, the Philistines (Palestinians), the Egyptians, the Assyrians/Babylonians (Iraq), Elam or Persia (Iran), Hamath (Syria), and the three nations of Edom, Moab, and Ammon, which are present-day Jordan. Even the ancient nation of Cush as present day Ethiopia is in the news because of civil war, famine, and its Black Jewish community which has recently been airlifted to Israel (65,000 people between 1985 and 1993). Can you appreciate how amazing this is? None of these groups are superpowers. How do they rate such attention? It is because the spotlight of history is not held in man's hand, but in the hand of God. He is the Director of the final act! He will do precisely what He has *always* said He would do!

There is another little known fact that is worth mentioning. There are Jewish people in virtually every nation and race. There are Chinese Jews, Indian Jews, Black Ethiopian Jews (as just mentioned), and Caucasian Jews. Some people believe that Jews are a distinct race of people when in fact they are ethnically plural. From ancient biblical times, a person of any race could join himself to Israel as a proselyte, such as Naomi's Moabite daughter-in-law Ruth or Moses' Ethiopian wife. A visit to modern Israel bears this out as you see Israelis from all over the earth. The salvation of God has always been open to those who would join themselves to Him from any nation.

> *Then I saw another angel flying in the midst of heaven, having the everlasting gospel to preach to those who dwell on the earth—to every nation, tribe, tongue, and people—saying with a loud voice, "Fear God and give glory to Him, for the hour of His judgment has come; and worship Him who made heaven and earth, the sea and springs of water"* (Revelation 14:6-7).

The Year 2000

Here we are near the year 2000, at least 6,000 years into recorded human history, and the nations we read about in the daily papers are the same as the nations we read of in the Bible. To ignore the fact of a logical plan is to err in understanding history. It is like looking at creation and saying there is no God and it all just happened by chance. There is a God and there is a God of history. Those who say that history is cyclical are the same ones who brought you the idea that man is just an advanced animal form with no created purpose or dignity. However, history is linear and God began history with His own initiative of creation and He will end temporal history on His own schedule, in what the Bible calls "the fullness of time."

The Fullness of Time

Certainly we are living in the time of fullness. It is evident in every category of contemporary activity. World population is exploding, the environment is overloaded, stress is at an all-time high, records are being broken in weather patterns of heat and cold, and wickedness is reaching the boiling point. Violence is on the rise and anarchy and rebellion are in vogue. All this is like a full cup that is about to overflow. "For behold, the darkness shall cover the earth, and deep darkness the people; but the Lord will arise over you, and His glory will be seen upon you" (Is. 60:2). As darkness spills out on the earth, we are seeing that this is one of the greatest periods of evangelism of all time. It is the final harvest time of world history.

Jesus had something specific to say in His parable of the wheat and tares regarding the time of harvest. In this parable, a man sowed good seed in his field, but in the night someone came and sowed tares (weeds) among the wheat. When the wheat sprouted and grew, tares also grew. "So the servants of the owner came and said to him, 'Sir, did you not sow good seed in your field? How then does it have tares?' He said to them, 'An enemy has done this' " (Matt. 13:27-28a). Before we continue, please notice that the owner's answer in the parable is God's answer for why there is evil in the world. There is an enemy of God called satan. He indeed has been at work sowing bad seed in the earth, which is growing up right beside the good seed of God's harvest. This fact makes the rest of the parable very pertinent to our day.

The servants said to him, "Do you want us then to go and gather them up?" But he said, "No, lest while you gather up the tares you also uproot the wheat with them. Let both grow together until the harvest, and at the time of harvest I will say to the reapers, 'First gather together the tares, and bind them in bundles to burn them, but gather the wheat into my barn' " (Matthew 13:28b-30).

The tares spoken of is a Middle Eastern plant that looks just like wheat when it is young. When it matures, however, the tares produce no grain while the wheat ripens fruitfully. Thus, there is a visible difference between the two mature plants and they can be safely separated without confusion. So it is with the maturing of prophecy. In the time of fullness, it all becomes clear.

It is interesting to note that the cause of fullness is the rain that falls on the earth. The rain brings forth the seeds that are in the ground, whether they be weeds or grain. As you know, rain is normally symbolic in Scripture of the outpouring of the Holy Spirit (as in Joel 2). It is also rain (and wind) that tests the foundations in the parable of the houses being built on rock or sand (see Mt. 7:25-27). I believe both of these examples indicate that the latter rain outpouring of the Holy Spirit is bringing the entire earth into fullness. Today wickedness (weeds) matures right along with righteousness (wheat) throughout society. So don't be surprised at the weeds that come up when the Holy Spirit moves in your personal life. God will deal with the weeds as you grow in Jesus.

We are living in the fullness of time when all these prophetic events are coming to pass right before our eyes. We will consider some of these areas in greater detail in the remaining chapters. Remember that this book is not simply a book about Israel, but is a testimony of the faithfulness of God. It is not only God's character that is faithful, but He has spoken it in a faithful word. The best part of all is that He will precisely bring to pass everything He has promised—both spiritually *and* physically. This is the time of fullness; the climax of history as we know it. It is harvest time—and are you ready for the grand finale? Are you ready for the Lord Jesus? Are you going to be included in the victory? We know the end of history: "And one cried to another and said; 'Holy, holy, holy is the Lord of hosts; the whole earth is full of His glory!' " (Isaiah 6:3) "For the earth will be filled with the knowledge of the glory of the Lord, as the waters cover the sea" (Habakkuk 12:14).

However, on the way to fullfilling His purpose, God still has a few obstacles to deal with. One of the most prominent of these is Islam. So what is Islam and what is God doing about it?

GOD IS FAITHFUL!

Chapter 13

The Baal Gods and Islam

The world's fastest growing religion, Islam, is on a collision course with destiny. "In 1984, Leon Uris explained that his purpose in writing *The Haj*, a novel, was to warn the West 'that we have an enraged bull of a billion people on our planet, and tilted the wrong way they could open the second road to Armageddon.' "(1) Another famous event involves the author Salman Rushdie, who was forced into permanent hiding because of death threats. His novel was supposedly blasphemous against Islam. What a curious form of book review: If you don't like the book, kill the author.

What kind of culture nurtures this type of violent environment? These threats were not from some fringe fanatic terrorist, but from the spiritual head of fundamentalist Islam, the ruler of Iran, a rising nation of great power in the Islamic world. With the diminished influence of Iraq after the Eight Year War with Iran (which claimed one million lives), and the Gulf War humiliation of Iraq by the West, Iran resumes its place as the leader of the militant masses of Islam. Dictators and Ayatollahs may rise and fall, yet the murderous spirit lives on in the next leader. Who are these people and where do they get the spirit that motivates them? Also, what do they believe and what is their intent? These are the questions answered in this chapter. *Who* they are examines their *roots*. *Where* they get their motivation examines their *spirit*. *What* they are examines their beliefs, and *why* they are examines their intentions.

The Roots of Islam

Islam is the name of the religion; its believers are known as Muslims. The common definition of the Arabic word *Islam* is submission. However, we need to understand that the idea of submission in their culture comes from the Koran, the Islamic bible or holy book. This submission is in direct contrast to the Christian and Jewish submission, which presupposes that the submission is *voluntary*. Islam demands submission in the sense of domination or control. *Imposed submission* is the fundamental non-negotiable lowest common denominator of Islam.

The majority of secular historians and sociologists consider Islam to be one of the world's three great monotheistic religions. In one sense this is true because they claim no god but Allah. But it gets confusing when there is the implication that Allah is the same "one" God who is worshiped by Jews and Christians. This error is repeated every day in today's media by inserting the word *God* in quotes from Arabic Muslim leaders like Saddam Hussein or Yassar Arafat. When they are speaking in Arabic, they are saying *Allah*, not God. If the media would use the word *Allah*, the reader would get an entirely different sense of what is actually being said in the quotation.

The traditional starting point for the roots of Islam is the establishment of a formal religion by Mohammed between

The Baal Gods and Islam

A.D. 613 and 624. This culminated in 625 with the conquering of Mecca and the beginning of his widespread acceptance as more than another desert warrior. I would like to follow the trail back further, however, for the spirit of Islam preceded the codification of the religion.

It is my belief that Allah is, in fact, one of the Baals or Baal gods that were the prominent deities of the pagans all through the Old Testament. That list of people includes the Canaanites, the Amalekites, and the Midianites, and all the way back to the Babylonians. The primary gods of Babylon, Marduk and Ishtar seemed to keep popping up in every pagan society under different names, but they were traceable to Babylon. In Canaan they were known as Moloch and Astarte, and together with Chomesh, Dagon, and other demonic "deities" were known as the Baals. I believe that the full name of Allah is Ba-Allah or Baal-lah. I have not been able to confirm this with documentation, so let it stand as a suggestion until it is confirmed.

There is, however, an amazing clue in the story of Gideon (circa 1200 B.C.). Gideon had seen the victory over the Midianites as the 120,000-man army turned on one another with the resulting death of 105,000. The two kings of Midian escaped with 15,000 troops, but were soon overtaken by Gideon and routed with the capture of the two kings. It is the death of the two kings that holds this fascinating clue, as recorded in Judges 8:21. "So Zebah and Zalmunna said, 'Rise yourself, and kill us; for as a man is, so is his strength.' So Gideon arose and killed Zebah and Zalmunna, and took the crescent ornaments that were on their camels' necks." It was not enough to simply kill them, but he took the "crescent ornaments" from the necks of their camels! Could this indicate a connection between their Baal worship and Islam? The crescent is the primary symbol of Islam.

Now let's go back a little further in time to about 2050 B.C. It is generally recognized by most historians that the Arab people descended from Ishmael. The name is as common among Moslems as Bill or Bob is among Americans, although the spelling varies (such as Ismail).

Historians say the original Arabs were a semi-nomadic, Semitic-speaking tribal people who dwelled in the northern section of the Arabian Peninsula, southeast of the Holy Land. The Bible records that the peoples who roamed the northern Arabian Desert area were largely the descendants of Abraham's firstborn son, Ishmael, and Isaac's son Esau, also known as Edom. God promised Abraham that He would make Ishmael a great nation, although He made clear that He would establish His covenant with Isaac (Gen. 17:20-21). The God of Israel also foretold that there would be enmity between the descendants of Isaac's twin sons, Jacob and Esau (Gen. 25:23). Esau's children began to fulfill that prophecy when they refused passage to the children of Israel who were on their way from Egypt to the Promised Land.(2)

It seems they are up to their old tricks again as we are witnessing the great second exodus from Russia and the Diaspora. Yet there is one other interesting mention of the Arabs in the return after the Babylonian captivity.

Arab/Jewish enmity was evident when the Jews returned to their homeland from the Babylonian Exile in the sixth and fifth centuries B.C. Arabs were apparently among the peoples who settled in the land during the exile, since they are listed as among those who were angry that returning Jews were rebuilding the destroyed walls of Jerusalem (Neh. 4:7). Earlier Nehemiah had told his opponents, including "Geshem the Arab," that God was behind the rebuilding project, adding that these Gentiles had "no heritage or right or memorial in Jerusalem" (Neh. 2:20).(3)

If this historical information gets a little tedious, please bear with it. We are establishing the consistent faithfulness of God throughout history. He has never wavered from His plan.

The Spirit of Islam

Spiritual demonic forces are infusing Islam today. These are pure paganism and occultism. There is no middle ground, no compromise with this bloodthirsty spirit; the bottom line is violent conquest. The fact that they say what we want to hear is actually a doctrine of lying. They are taught that lying is a righteous way to achieve a desired effect for Islam and they will be rewarded for their "successful" lie. If you understand this, it is a lot easier to understand their love of the Western media. They just tell us what we want to hear while going about their secretive purposes. An example of this was when Yassar Arafat "renounced terrorism" because the U.S. required it as a pre-condition of initiating direct dialogue with us. Within a short time he was proven to be behind several new acts of terrorism. We were very indignant, for we did not understand Islam. But he did not decide to stop terrorism; he simply agreed to "say" he would stop. To him it was not even a conflict of logic! Will our State Department ever learn this lesson? However, his "lying spirit" is just the tip of the iceberg.

The major demonic principality behind Islam is Moloch, (or Marduk), the Babylonian and Canaanite Baal god. In our search for biblical answers concerning Israel's right to the land, it is good to know why the previous (Canaanite) inhabitants were dispossessed of their rights to it. You may recall it was the worship of this deity and its pagan relatives that was the original reason for the Canaanites being kicked out of the Holy Land, as stated in Deuteronomy 18:9-12:

> *When you come into the land which the Lord your God is giving you, you shall not learn to follow the abominations of those nations. There shall not be found among you anyone who makes his son or his daughter pass through the fire, or one who practices witchcraft, or a soothsayer, or one who interprets omens, or a sorcerer, or one who conjures spells, or a medium, or a spiritist, or one who calls up the dead. For all who do these things are an abomination to the Lord, and because of these abominations the Lord your God drives them out from before you.*

Who was this pagan god who demanded child sacrifice (passing through the fire)? We need to examine Moloch a little closer.

> A wide variety of practices is cited. An "enchanter" is a whisperer or snake charmer; a witch, one who uses charms or spells; a wizard, one who claimed to know the secrets of the other world; a necromancer, one who inquires of the dead, and so on. But the key evil is Molech worship. The word Moloch (or Melech, Melek, or Malik), meaning **king**, is a misvocalization of the name of a pagan, the consonants of **king** being retained and the vowels of **shame** used. Human sacrifice was made to this god, who is identified as the god of Ammon in I Kings 11:7,33. "Molech" is "the king" or "kingship." The name of Moloch is also

The Baal Gods and Islam

given as Milcom (I Kings 6:5,33) and Malcam (Jer. 49:1,3 RV; Zeph. 1:5). Moloch was an aspect of Baal (Jer. 32:35), **Baal** meaning **lord**. Under the name of Melcarth, king of Tyre, Baal was worshipped with human sacrifices at Tyre.

Since Moloch represented kingship and power, sacrifices to Moloch represented the purchase, at the very least, of immunity or insurance and protection, and, at its highest claim, of power. The "higher" sacrifices in paganism, and especially Baal worship, were sacrifices of humanity, i.e., self-mutilations, notably castration, the sacrifice of children or of posterity, and the like. The priest became identified with the god to the degree that he "departed" from humanity by his castration, his separation from normal human relationships, and his abnormalities. The king became identified with the god to the degree that he manifested absolute power. The sacrifice of children was the supreme sacrifice to Moloch.(4)

What kind of a god was Moloch? He was the god of the sacrifice of newborn babies. This was the central act of his worship; the firstborn of every woman's body had to be sacrificed to Moloch. According to one tradition, there was an opening at the back of the brazen idol, and after a fire was made within it, each parent had to come and with his own hands place his firstborn child in the white-hot, outstretched hands of Molech. According to this tradition, the parent was not allowed to show emotion, and drums were beaten so that the baby's cries could not be heard as the baby died in the hands of Molech. And there, I would say, stand many in our day. Many of those who come to me, those with whom I work, are the children destroyed by a worse than Molech. Men—men who were supposedly the men of God—have stood by while their children were eaten up by modern theology. And then we are told that there is supposed to be no emotion shown.

Some of you who read this bear yourselves the marks of these things from the background from which you come. All of us are marked by this in some way, to some extent, because our Western, post-Christian world has been undercut by this liberal theology. Every scar this present generation has, every tear cried, every baby which some of you who read this have willfully aborted, every drug trip you have taken cannot be separated from the fact that the church has turned away and become unfaithful. This generation are the babies in the hands of Molech.(5)

The analogy between Moloch and abortion deserves further thought, but it is not within the scope of this book. Let us end this section on the spirit of Islam with a more specific look at the connections of the occult to Islam with a quotation from Professor Peter A. Michas:

Even before Islam was formed by Mohammed, the Arabian tribes had a custom of traveling to Mecca and worshipping a strange cube of black rock called the "ka'abba," which some scholars believe to be a meteorite. Later, when Judean folklore began to take hold among the nomads, some old-wives stories began circulating among the primitive Arab tribes. They were told that this rock "had been raised by Adam, destroyed by the flood, and rebuilt by Abraham with the help of his son Ishmael, the father of all Arabs." These fables were incorporated into Islam. Today this stone may be found in the corner of the central mosque in Mecca. According to another Koranic legend, it fell from paradise during the reconstruction of the Temple. The god of this stone in the old pagan Ka'abba religion was called Allah. A spirit of that same name spoke to the founder of Islam in visions, and he adopted the name for his god.

Mohammed invaded and conquered Mecca. The superstitious natives believed that such a victory was divinely inspired, and duly gave him their allegiance. There Mohammed denounced the plurality of gods, and proclaimed the sole deity of Allah. All human beings, he said, must be (in literal translation) the "slaves of Allah," which is also the meaning of the term "Islam." A "Moslem" is "one who submits." Further, the Islamic term for "peace" ("salaam") also means "to submit." Mohammed's view of world peace was a world totally dominated and submissive to the rule of Islam. Today, Islamic radicals still believe in world conquest—ruled by Islamic dictatorships governed by the *sharia*, Islam's barbaric Cannon law. — As for the pagan customs of his people, he incorporated many of them into his religion. Indeed, the concepts of honorable blood-shedding, shame and the sacred vendetta, or blood-feud, were made holy. Mohammed—the offspring of a violent, savage heritage—could not understand the vital importance of the concept of peace and coexistence that underlines both Christianity and Judaism. True to his legacy he conceived a religion of warfare and struggle, in which the war was holy (*jihad*) and tolerance baneful, and in which the very meaning of the word "peace" came to mean not cooperation and the acceptance of others, but precisely the opposite—the total destruction (or submission) of the enemy. Even today, Islamic terrorists use the word "peace" when communicating with the West. However, "peace" has a very different meaning to a religious Moslem.(6)

Now that we have caught a glimpse of the violent spirit of Moloch that is behind Islam, what do Muslims actually believe?

The Beliefs of Islam

I mentioned earlier that the desert god Allah is a different god than the God of Israel, the God of Abraham, Isaac, and Jacob. I believe, in fact, that Islam is a counterfeit religion of Judaism and Christianity. We will now examine facts to confirm that point. Also modern Islam has to answer for and defend its own holy book, the Koran. So in this section we will look at some of the claims of the Koran in the light of the Bible. First, though, let us hear what Derek Prince teaches on the subject.

> The strongest spiritual force that opposes God's purposes and God's people in the Middle East today is Islam, the Mohammedan religion. Yet Mohammed, the founder of Islam, was a false prophet. As such, his words and the movement he brought into being will ultimately be brought to naught. Some may be inclined to challenge the statement that Mohammed was a false prophet. To this I would offer one brief and simple response: *If Jesus was a true prophet, then Mohammed was a false prophet.* Following are a few of the main points in which the teaching of Mohammed contradicts that of Jesus.
>
> 1. Jesus declared that He was the Son of God. Islam totally rejects the idea that God can have a son, dismissing it as

blasphemy. Islam further rejects the concept of one God revealed in three Persons.

2. Historically, the Christian faith has centered around the crucifixion and resurrection of Jesus, Islam denies that Jesus ever actually died on the cross, or that He was resurrected.

3. Jesus claimed He had come to fulfill the Law and the prophets (Matt. 5:17). Islam claims that it alone is the true fulfillment and completion of the revelation contained in the Old and New Testaments.

4. Jesus promised His followers that He would send them "another Comforter" (John 14:15-17,26, KJV). The Christian Church has always taught that this promise was fulfilled by the coming of the Holy Spirit on the Day of Pentecost. Islam claims that Mohammed was the Comforter promised by Jesus.

5. The Old Testament, which Jesus accepted as authoritative, states clearly that Abraham offered his son Isaac on the altar on Mount Moriah (Gen. 22:9-12). Islam claims that Ishmael was the son whom Abraham offered.

The direct opposition of the teaching of Mohammed to that of Jesus is mirrored at large in the contemporary world situation, and particularly in the Middle East. There is a single, spiritual force that unites the nations of the Middle East in fierce, unyielding opposition to the outworking of God's purposes for Israel: *it is Islam.*(7)

The fact that they deny Jesus' death means they have no basis for forgiveness according to Hebrews 9:22: "And according to the law almost all things are purified with blood, and without shedding of blood there is no remission." By denying the blood sacrifice of Jesus once and for all for all who believe, they must live in their sins. Now let's look at some quotes from the Koran by David Dolan.

> The Islamic holy book urges all Muslims to "make war" on the unbelievers "until idolatry is no more and Allah's religion reigns supreme" (Sura 8:39). The reward for dying in a jihad struggle is instantaneous entrance into paradise, which the Koran makes clear is a place of great sensual pleasure. Modern Muslim apologists maintain that jihad does not necessarily mean actual fighting. Jihad is also waged by nonviolent struggle through education, propaganda and economic boycott. But it is abundantly clear from the Koran (and from the *Hadith*, the codified Islamic oral tradition of Mohammed's actions and sayings) that the *primary* meaning of *jihad* is actual fighting—"holy war." That is why Islam has long been known as the religion of the sword. ...Conversion to Islam was a very simple matter, as it is today. One had only to recite three times the *Shahada*, the Islamic Affirmation of Faith: "There is no God but Allah, and Mohammed is the Prophet of Allah."
>
> According to the Koran, Jesus is not the Son of God, but "the son of Mary," since God could not have a son. Those who declare that Jesus is God are "unbelievers" who will be "forbidden entrance into Paradise, and shall be cast into the fire of hell," for "the Messiah, the son of Mary, was no more than an apostle" (Sura 5:73-75). The Koran's version of the birth of Jesus is very different from the Gospel accounts. In Sura Mary (*Sura* means "revelation"), the Holy Spirit is sent to Mary in the form of a full-grown man who tells the frightened Jewish maiden that he has "come to give you a holy son" (15-20). The Koranic account then

reveals that Jesus came into the world while Mary rested under a palm tree somewhere in "the east." Suddenly a voice comes "from below" her, apparently the newborn baby Jesus, who tells Mary to shake the tree and eat of its fruit (24-27). Later the infant surprises Mary's relatives by speaking from his cradle, saying, "I am the servant of Allah," and describing his mission on earth. The Koran then reveals that "this is the whole truth, which they (apparently the Christians and Jews) are unwilling to accept," adding that "Allah forbid that He Himself should beget a son!" (29-36). ... "Say: Praise be to Allah who has never begotten a son, who has no partner in His kingdom" (Sura 17:111)."(8)

Those last two quotes from the Koran are among dozens of similar quotes, denying the Sonship of Jesus, that are written in two-foot-high Arabic letters around the inside of the Dome of the Rock, the Muslim shrine on the Temple Mount in Jerusalem. Perhaps you now have a better understanding of the real reasons for the conflicts in the Middle East. Now, let's turn to the last question: Why are they still here?

The Intentions of Islam

Their intentions should be plain by now. Islam intends to dominate the entire world. Their theology allows for nothing else.

To this day, it is a cardinal tenet of Islam to divide the world into two irreconcilable camps, the *dar al-Islam* or "house of Islam", which includes all countries where Islam currently prevails, and the *dar al-harb* or "house of war", which includes everywhere else. The object of Islam and its promoters is to expand their power until all is within their realm. It is a global vision, similar to that used until recently by Communism, but more powerful because it is a religion, not a political ideology.(9)

The rule of Christians is only tolerated. The rule of Jews, especially in the "Arab Middle East," is intolerable. In either case they view the situation as temporary, as only a matter of time.

The late Iranian leader Ayatollah Khomeini taught that Satan created "that cancerous tumor" Israel, with Allah's approval, as a judgment on backslidden Muslim nations. When Muslims, especially decadent Western-inspired leaders, repent of their wicked ways, then Allah will destroy the "infidel" state. To say the least, this view—widely believed by Palestinians—greatly impedes efforts to establish a lasting peace between the Muslim world and Israel.(10)

Iranian leader Ayatollah Khameini, speaking on June 4, 1990—the first anniversary of his predecessor Ayatollah Khomeini's death—Khameini vowed that Iran will not rest until Israel is destroyed.(11)

Obviously, the Middle East, and indeed the world, is on a collision course with destiny. The problem for Islam is that it clashes with the world on both ends of the spectrum. As we have seen, Muslims clash with the Bible and its followers. But they also have a major contradiction with the New Agers of the new world order of humanism because Islam's most adamant pillar of faith is "No god but Allah." This kind of intolerance will not be allowed in this new order where any religion will be encouraged as long as it does not claim it is the only way to God. This Islamic religious intolerance will be outlawed

The Baal Gods and Islam

because it limits "freedom of religion." Of course, this is a point that will also conflict with true Christianity because of Jesus' words in John 14:6: "Jesus said to him, 'I am the way, the truth, and the life. No one comes to the Father except through Me.'"

The booming Muslim population of one billion is adding to the pressure. According to Daniel Pipes, writing in the *National Review*:

> They constitute more than 85 per cent of the population in some 32 countries. ... According to a study by John R. Weeks, countries with large numbers of Muslims have a total fertility rate of six children per Muslim woman, compared to 1.7 per woman in the developed countries.(12)

Something will have to happen sooner or later, but the interesting thing is that I don't see Islam lasting. There is a long history of infighting and inability to act in unity. In the end, it will be their downfall. Daniel Pipes continues:

> Further, Muslims are not now politically unified and never will be so. They are in the throes of working out conflicting nationalist claims (Lebanon and Syria), divergent ideological programs (Syria and Iraq), overlapping territorial claims (Iraq and Iran), contrasting religious visions (Iran and Saudi Arabia), and so forth. Arab unity has failed, as have the other schemes to bind Muslims together politically.(13)

Of course we have previously pointed out the biblical reasons for "enmity" among the Arabs, so I agree with Mr. Pipes.

This disunity is visible at any level. Just look at the PLO and HAMAS, two competing terrorist groups vying for the right to represent the Palestinians in Israel (who would be better off under the Israelis). The Intifada struggle in Israel for some months now has registered more deaths from infighting among the PLO and HAMAS than at the hands of the Israelis. The PLO has decided to accept a peace treaty that would give them a legal foothold in the West Bank. The PLO "incremental plan" would have them take over Israel parcel by parcel until, as the PLO Charter says, (which they have never renounced), they drive Israel into the sea.

Yassar Arafat, still the head of the PLO as of this writing, has claimed to be a descendant of the Philistines. Although this is almost totally impossible historically, it is in fact true in that he does seem to have the spirit and methods of the Philistines (marauding raids of terror). I have pointed out earlier that the Hebrew word for Palestinians and for Philistines is identical, so maybe the spirit in Arafat is the same one that was prevalent in biblical times. At any rate, the Bible does have the last word in Amos 1:8: " 'I will cut off the inhabitant from Ashdod, and the one who holds the scepter from Ashkelon; I will turn My hand against Ekron, and the remnant of the Philistines shall perish,' says the Lord God." If they are still around, their days are numbered!

Hamas, on the other hand, is worse. They are sponsored by Iran and are fundamentalists dedicated to the destruction of Israel. The meaning of their name in Hebrew is "violence." It is the exact word used in Genesis 6:13: "And God said to Noah, 'The end of all flesh has come before Me, for the earth is filled with violence through them; and behold, I will destroy them with the earth.' " David Dolan has an interesting quote from the Hamas Covenant:

The Baal Gods and Islam

Article 6 says HAMAS is "working to unfurl the banner of Allah over every inch of Palestine." Article 8 endorses martyrdom in the name of the holy jihad: "Allah is the ultimate objective of HAMAS, his messenger Mohammed its touchstone, the Koran its constitution, 'jihad' its path, and death for the sake of Allah its chief interest." Article 13 states that — "There is no solution to the Palestinian problem except through 'jihad'."(14)

What about the salvation of the Arabs? Is there any hope for them? Or are they so bound in Islam that they will never find Jesus?

"The Palestinian Arabs are definitely victims — but not primarily of the Israelis. They are, in my opinion, mainly the victims of an often-violent religion based on a corruption of the Bible. While I have great love and respect for the Muslims as people made in the image of God, I cannot but grieve for them as prisoners of a religious system, based on the Koran and Hadith, which exalts warfare and almost mandates hatred, or at least scorn, of the Jews.(15)

The Bible says that those who live by the sword will die by it (Mt. 26:52). But Lance Lambert, (an Israeli believer, Bible teacher, and author) gave a scenario that does offer a ray of hope. He was speaking at the International Intercessors Conference in Jerusalem in January 1990, which I attended. He believes that radical Islam is going to experience utter failure in its aims, and then in complete and total disillusionment, those who are willing will turn to the Messiah Jesus of Israel and be saved.

Those who believe that the Church replaced Israel and became God's second wife should understand that Islam believes

Prophesy to the Land

it has replaced both Israel and the Church! God has never had another bride and never will. There is only one groom and only one bride. All who believe in Jesus are part of the bride, whether it was ancient Jews looking ahead in faith, or believers who look back in history to Jesus' sacrifice in faith. Of course Muslims can be saved if they turn from Allah and accept the God of Abraham, Isaac, and Jacob, accepting Jesus as the Son of God.

Philippians 2:10-11 says every knee will bow and every tongue will confess the Lordship of Jesus, to the glory of God the Father. This does not mean all will be saved. It does mean all will bow and acknowledge that Jesus is in fact the Lord. They will either do it as those who are saved, with great joy and giving of thanks, or with total despair and defeat as the conquered enemy of God. But there is one thing for sure—there will be former Muslims saved and rejoicing with the rest of us. "And they sang a new song, saying: 'You are worthy to take the scroll, and to open its seals; for You were slain, and have redeemed us to God by Your blood Out of every tribe and tongue and people and nation' " (Rev. 5:9). Pray for the salvation of some from "every tribe," all people in the awful grip of Islam, that God will have mercy and reveal Jesus to them before it is too late.

God's judgments are sometimes greater on those He has chosen, as we will see as we turn our attention back to Israel.

GOD IS FAITHFUL!

Chapter 14

Seeing Double Double

There is a great line in the movie *Fiddler on the Roof* where the main character, Tevye, poignantly questions his Jewishness in a casual prayer conversation with God. "I know we are the chosen people, but just once, couldn't you choose someone else?" Though there is some resentment, denial, and even jealousy among other nations regarding the "chosen people" tag, we need to examine in this chapter the deeper implications of being chosen. Israel has the ultimate "favored nation" status of God: "For thus says the Lord of hosts: 'He sent Me after glory, to the nations which plunder you; for he who touches you touches the apple of His eye' " (Zech. 2:8). Although it is logical to assume that this means special blessings and favor from God, it also includes greater responsibility and accountability as Tevye bemoaned in his movie prayer. Jesus also invoked this principle. There are several concrete examples from the Bible of this special status of Israel causing double attention from God in judgment as well as in blessing.

First, let us review the promised blessing articulated in Deuteronomy 7:6-9:

For you are a holy people to the Lord your God; the Lord your God has chosen you to be a people for Himself, a special treasure above all the peoples on the face of the earth. The Lord did not set His love on you nor choose you because you were more in number than any other people, for you were the least of all peoples; but because the Lord loves you, and because He would keep the oath which He swore to your fathers, the Lord has brought you out with a mighty hand, and redeemed you from the house of bondage, from the hand of Pharaoh king of Egypt. Therefore know that the Lord your God, He is God, the faithful God who keeps covenant and mercy for a thousand generations with those who love Him and keep His commandments.

Notice that God keeps His word for a thousand generations; if one generation is 40 years, then that would equal 40,000 years! Also, please notice that God's choice of Israel was not because of some innate value or greatness of size. He chose them because of His own love and because of His oath to their fathers. This passage continues to outline the blessings of obedience and the curses or judgments of disobeying the Lord's commands. It is important to recognize that being chosen eternally does not exempt a person or a nation from the consequences of sin.

The profound point I am trying to make is that God's choice of Israel not only brings great blessing, but also great scrutiny. This principle is also in the New Testament in Luke 12:48: "But he who did not know, yet committed things deserving of stripes, shall be beaten with few. For everyone to whom much is given, from him much will be required; and to whom much has been committed, of him they will ask the more." Since more was given to Israel than to the other nations, more was required. Double blessings also means double judgment. Read this passage in Jeremiah 16:18: "And first I will repay double for their iniquity and their sin, because they have defiled My land; they have filled My inheritance with the carcasses of their detestable and abominable idols." Please notice the fact that God will repay Israel *double* for all their sin! Which of us has even paid for our own sins singly, let alone doubly! We could not begin to pay for our own sins, which is why we have received the sacrifice of Messiah Jesus as the full payment for our sins. This is an awesome fact, that God requires double for Israel's sins.

Now there is a certain balance achieved with this point when we realize that along with this double scrutiny by God comes a sort of double protection. We saw this earlier in the verse that spoke of how the person who touches Israel touches the apple of God's eye. God will act quickly and strongly on behalf of His beloved nation toward any who touch her. Remember the promise to Abram? "I will bless those who bless you, and I will curse him who curses you; and in you all the families of the earth shall be blessed" (Gen. 12:3). There is another clear support of this point found in Jeremiah 17:18: "Let them be ashamed who persecute me, but do not let me be put to shame; let them be dismayed, but do not let me be dismayed. Bring on them the day of doom, and destroy them with double destruction!" The enemies of God's people are in danger of *double destruction*!

Prophesy to the Land

This idea of God's judgment against Israel's enemies is strongly emphasized in Psalm 83. In verses 4 and 5, their *goal* is revealed to be the same as the goal of militant Arabs and Palestinians today. "They have said, 'Come, and let us cut them off from being a nation, that the name of Israel may be remembered no more.' For they have consulted together with one consent; they form a confederacy against You" (Ps.83:4-5). The *alliance* members are listed in verses six through eight.

The tents of Edom and the Ishmaelites; Moab and the Hagrites; Gebal, Ammon, and Amalek; Philistia with the inhabitants of Tyre; Assyria also has joined with them; they have helped the children of Lot. Selah (Psalm 83:6-8).

These names include the following modern peoples: Jordan and the Arabs in general; the Palestinians; the people of Syria, Iraq, Iran, Saudia Arabia, and Lebanon. This is an amazing roll call of most of today's militant Arab nations. Their *motive* then is revealed in verse 12. "Who said, 'Let us take for ourselves the pastures of God for a possession.' " Notice that this is not only coveting of Israel's land, but actually includes the idea of stealing from God! Their rebellion from God is behind everything else.

So far, we have seen that because of being specially chosen by God, Israel has had double blessings, double judgments, and double protection. Her double penalty for sin can be seen historically in many cases where God allowed Israel's enemies to overcome and enslave her people in Egypt, Assyria, Babylon, and even in their own land by the Romans. In each case, except Rome, they subsequently repented, returned to God, and were restored to their land in at least a remnant company.

Seeing Double Double

This was not the case however, after they rejected the Messiah. Then they were scattered among all the nations of the earth where they were persecuted relentlessly and without mercy for nearly 2,000 years! "Remember, I pray, the word that You commanded Your servant Moses, saying: 'If you are unfaithful, I will scatter you among the nations' " (Neh. 1:8). The Spanish Inquisition, the Dark Ages, and most horribly, the Holocaust slaughter of six million Jews, are just an overview of the evidence of history. During the Dark Ages, the Jews were actually blamed for the "Black Death" of the bubonic plague.

> The scourge, which wiped out a third of the continent's population (including, of course, Jews) between 1347 and 1350, was blamed by the masses on the Jews. They had become the usual scapegoat for anything that went wrong. The populace believed that the Jews had poisoned Europe's water supplies with a concoction of sacred hosts, human hearts, and various insects and animals. Untold thousands of Jews were massacred in southern France, Spain, Switzerland, Germany, Austria, Poland, and Belgium because of this ridiculous charge. More than two hundred Jewish communities were entirely wiped out. To his credit, Pope Clement VI tried to stop the carnage, but he could not.(1)

This does not even begin to recall the individual stories of suffering that could be told case by case. They truly have paid double for their sins! Would you or I like to trade places with them in their historical judgments? As I have already stated, we cannot even pay singly for our sins. When speaking publicly about God's wrath and righteous judgment, I often ask: "How many of you, if given the choice between justice and mercy, would choose justice? That is, do you really want God to give you exactly what you deserve? As for me, I desire mercy." When put that way, most people see the point and choose mercy. Yet the Bible itself says that the Jewish people have received double for all their sins. Think of it!

This shocking and depressing knowledge would begin to seem eternally unfair if it were not for the end of the story. God does not reject them forever. His plan includes forgiveness and restoration. Isaiah saw it and prophesied comfort: "Speak comfort to Jerusalem, and cry out to her, that her warfare is ended, that her iniquity is pardoned; for she has received from the Lord's hand double for all her sins" (Is. 40:2). There is a time coming when God will pardon her and pronounce that she has paid double for her sins. We now know of the provision for the Jews' forgiveness, along with our own, through the blood of the Lamb, Jesus. Yet there is still a limitation on Israel because God has blinded their eyes. "Just as it is written: 'God has given them a spirit of stupor, eyes that they should not see and ears that they should not hear, to this very day' " (Rom. 11:8). They also have been banned from ruling Jerusalem until a specific time at the end of the age. Jesus Himself speaks of this fact in Luke 21:24, stating that Jerusalem will be trampled by the nations until the time of the Gentiles is fulfilled. It is then that the timing of Israel's restoration is brought to pass.

Zechariah also saw this restoration in light of the "double" principle in Zechariah 9:12: "Return to the stronghold, you prisoners of hope. Even today I declare that I will restore double to you." Seeing this reference in the context of the prophecy of the Messiah in verse 9 makes it even more interesting: "Rejoice greatly, O daughter of Zion! Shout, O daughter of Jerusalem! Behold, your King is coming to you; He is just and having salvation, lowly and riding on a donkey, a colt, the foal of a donkey" (Zech. 9:9). And here is one more verse that needs to be considered, Isaiah 61:7: "Instead of your shame you shall have double honor, and instead of confusion they shall rejoice in their portion. Therefore in their land they shall possess double; everlasting joy shall be theirs." Again the context is important. This is the great passage of Isaiah 61 that Jesus quoted in the synagogue in Nazareth in Luke 4. Now you may remember Jesus said the passage was fulfilled *that* day in their hearing. This is not a contradiction; He stopped reading just before these verses:

And they shall rebuild the old ruins, they shall raise up the former desolations, and they shall repair the ruined cities, the desolations of many generations. Strangers shall stand and feed your flocks, and the sons of the foreigner shall be your plowmen and your vinedressers. But you shall be named the priests of the Lord, they shall call you the servants of our God. You shall eat the riches of the Gentiles, and in their glory you shall boast. Instead of your shame you shall have double honor, and instead of confusion they shall rejoice in their portion. Therefore in their land they shall possess double; everlasting joy shall be theirs (Isaiah 61:4-7).

Jesus left out those verses because their fulfillment was not for *that* day! We are now, almost 2,000 years later, living in the day of the fulfillment of the rest of the context. Praise the Lord! There is no mistaking the specific land covenant words. Instead of their shame, they will have *double honor* and they will *possess double* in their *land*!

Finally, there is one other "double" that applies to modern Israel—the *double standard*. Atrocities occur regularly in the totalitarian Arab countries—such as the Iraqi chemical poison gassing of the Kurds. These events usually escape media attention because the society in those countries is generally closed to the free press. How much, for example, do you know about the "east bank" of the Jordan River? Because all the attention is on the West Bank, you would think it is the only river in the world with only one bank! Yet the conditions in the refugee camps in Jordan are much worse than those in Israeli territory. But the media does not have the same access in Jordan.

> The most subtle way the media and the international community have propagated this myth, is by unequivocally describing Judea, Samaria and Gaza as "the occupied territories". This ominous and misleading phrase has fed anti-Israel propaganda for the past 25 years.
>
> According to international law, an occupying power is a state which holds territory taken from its legitimate sovereign in an act of aggression. But what few people know is that Egypt was not the legitimate sovereign of the Gaza Strip in 1967, nor was Jordan the legitimate sovereign of the West Bank. Both countries seized these territories illegally during the war of aggression against Israel in 1948. Egypt never claimed Gaza as part of its territory, and Jordan's annexation of the West Bank was not internationally recognized. What is more, Israel did not take these territories in an act of aggression; Israel was threatened and attacked from these territories and not the other way around.
>
> Furthermore, most nations in the world today have had their boundaries drawn and redrawn as a result of war. The

Seeing Double Double

U.S., for example, would never return land to Mexico or the Indians. And after World War 2, Germany's neighbors redrew their borders to prevent more Germany aggression in the future. Israel, however, is asked to do what other nations are not, because it is judged by a *double standard*. (Emphasis mine.)(2)

When President Assad, the dictator of Syria, had 10.000 to 25,000 of his own people massacred in February 1982, it was not known at all to the world media until much later.

Amnesty International, in its November 1983 report on Syria, said estimates ranged from 10,000 to 25,000 dead... The Syrian regime of President Hafez al-Assad, which was responsible for carrying out the massacre, did little to dispute these figures.(3)

Yet in Israel, when young Palestinian boys throw stones and bottles at the Israeli Defense Forces, every major and many minor news organizations in the world descend on Israel like a horde of locusts, catching every incident on videotape. I am not at all defending the actions of the Israelis. I am just pointing out that there is a *double standard* in the way Israel is viewed and judged by the world media, compared to their Arab and Palestinian cousins. I also want to make it clear that I am not complaining about this inequity; it is part of the sovereign purpose of God in bringing His beloved people to the place of repentance and their inevitable restoration not only to their land, but to their God.

So we have seen that the double principle works two ways: for and against Israel. They have double promises, double protection, double judgments, and double rewards. In light of this discussion, we may or may not like what we have discovered, but we can hardly deny the fact of Israel's special place in the purposes of God for His creation. God's own personal integrity is at stake and He will certainly always keep His word.

GOD IS FAITHFUL!

Chapter 15

Tears

An Eyewitness Account of the Holocaust

Note: The following is an eyewitness report from Lawrence Fuller of Clearwater, Florida. He is my wife's uncle and has always found it difficult to relive those dark days of World War II. His eyewitness account is included here because of the growing problem of *denial* over the years. There is an increasing number of young people who doubt the Holocaust. Israel has a completely documented Holocaust memorial museum in Jerusalem called Yad Vashem. Also, a profound new Holocaust museum has just been completed in Washington D.C. This chapter is my small part in preserving the historical truth. It is with deep respect and gratitude that I present Mr. Fuller's personal recollection of that unforgettable event.

* * *

This is an account of one of the most significant and shocking days of my life. It is a testimony of things I saw and how I felt on a special day in April 1945. After 45 years, some of the

Prophesy to the Land

minor details and numbers quoted that day have left my memory, but what I saw in a few hours, I remember vividly to this day.

I answered the call to serve in the U.S. Army in the spring of 1943. After a vigorous training program I was assigned to the 131st Ordinance Heavy Maintenance Company. When special overseas training was complete, we were shipped to France as a unit in the late summer of 1944. This was after the great Normandy invasion, but before the French harbors were cleared of battle refuse.

Our company was unattached to any particular division at first, but we moved steadily across France, servicing various mechanized units as the German army retreated gradually back to its homeland. Our duty was to repair all Army equipment and to keep all the fighting units moving. Our company had trained personnel and equipment to repair everything from a watch to the largest tanks, trucks, and tractors.

Suddenly, after arriving in Nancy, France, we were designated to assist General George S. Patton and his armored division as they moved north to Luxembourg and Belgium where the Battle of the Bulge was taking place. Heavy fighting took place all winter with little advance until spring, when General Patton's troops thrust deeply into Germany.

Finally in early April we set up shop in a large field some 15 or 20 miles from the city of Weimer. Just a few miles beyond this city was a place known as "Camp Buchenwald." Our high command knew about this place, but most of the troops knew little or nothing about it. The orders had been given to the tank units to make a run toward Buchenwald and to capture it as quickly as possible and as intact as possible.

Tears

A bitter battle took place as Hitler's army tried to hold off the American troops. They tried to buy time for the S.S. troops and guards to destroy the camp before the Americans arrived. However, our commanders seemed to be aware of their tactics and applied such overwhelming firepower that the mission was accomplished quickly. When our tanks rumbled up to the main gate of this terrible place, our men were aghast at what they saw.

The German commander of the camp had tried to destroy the whole place with sort of a "scorched earth" policy. His intent was to kill all the inmates, then burn all the buildings; instead, they ran out of time and had to flee for their lives as the American tanks approached the camp. They had been confident that their troops could hold off our tanks, but they waited too long. Thus several thousand lives were spared with the liberation of this camp.

The very next day, the orders went out to all American units in the area for as many men as possible to come to the camp to inspect the place. Our company responded and sent two 6X6 trucks with about 40 men. We all wondered why we were being sent there.

Upon arrival we were gathered into a group for instructions. We were told that we were about to witness a terrible atrocity. The officers in charge wanted as many men as possible to see what had been found there. They told us they wanted the world to know the truth and for us to fix in our minds and never forget what we were about to see. They need not have worried, for what I saw was so horrible I could never forget. It is still a vivid memory.

Buchenwald was a notorious concentration camp in the heart of Germany. Although not as many were killed here, as in some other death camps like Auchswitz in Poland, it was the final destination for thousands of innocent people. Most of the inmates were Jews, but many others died here as a result of their political or religious views that posed a threat to Hitler. I will attempt to convey to you some of the horror of this place and some of the feelings that swept over us as we witnessed the atrocities that had taken place for several years. The following is not a pretty picture.

We were broken into groups of about a dozen men each and were told not to offer any inmate any food or candy. These people were so starved that they might even kill each other for a piece of candy. We were also told that the International Red Cross was on its way to care for these people.

A little, dark-haired Jewish inmate guided our group around. He was probably about 30 years old and spoke enough English for us to understand very well. He seemed reasonably healthy but really was only skin and bones—he probably weighed no more than 100 pounds.

He first showed us an open lot near the front gate. This was an assembly area for the prisoners, where they were called together for orders and sometimes punishment in the whipping rack that stood in front of the area. This was like a board wall with holes through which they would secure the person's head and hands. They would then be beaten on the back and buttocks with a whip or rod. Our guide said that some prisoners were beaten the first day in camp, just to break their spirits. Anyone who tried to escape, refused to work, or broke any rule of the camp, was punished here. Attempting to escape usually meant death.

We then went to one of the many barrack-type buildings where they lived. There were many of these buildings to house

Tears

the thousands of prisoners. These barracks were about 100 feet long and about 25 feet wide. Along each side there were three shelves about six feet deep. The bottom one was a few inches off the floor with the others about 3 feet above the one below. About every 6 feet was a divider, thus creating a series of cubicles along each side of the building. Four men were assigned to sleep in each cubicle with no pad, pillow, or blanket. Four men sleeping in a cubicle 6' X 6' X 3' necessitated them to all sleep on their sides. When one turned over, they all had to turn. In cold winter weather, they had one thin blanket per cubicle. There were deep hollow places worn into the boards where prisoners' hips and shoulders had lain there over the years. Our guide showed us huge calluses on his hips after sleeping this way for the year that he had been there.

Next, we went to one of the yards where hundreds of prisoners were out in the sun. This was a sunny spring day. The look of hopelessness and despair was beyond belief. All were dressed in gray striped prison garb which resembled loose pajamas made from mattress covers. These men showed no emotion. Many looked near death. They were sick and dirty. Most looked like skeletons with eyes sunken and no expression. Some had dysentery so bad that they had no control of their bowels and had abandoned their clothes completely. It was indeed a wretched, horrible sight.

There was one water faucet in the yard for four or five barracks. This was turned on for only about 2 hours per day. This meant that about 800 men had to draw what they needed for drinking and bathing in this short time or they got none. Many were too sick to get to the faucet. As we looked with shock at what we were seeing, we all began to realize how horrible

Buchenwald really was. But it got worse as we continued to explore the place.

Our guide then took us to the work area, where they had to labor until too sick to do so. This was like a warehouse built close to the living area so the Allied planes would not bomb it. Munitions of many types had been assembled here—small but important parts for the German war machine.

Our next stop was the camp hospital. The rooms were clean and painted white, but in reality it was not there to help the sick. It was more like a laboratory. Prisoners were brought here on the pretext of being treated, but most were experimented with. Few ever left alive. However, with a clean bed, decent food, and no work, most of them felt fortunate to be taken there. Yes, there was a section where simple things like colds and fevers were treated with prisoners reporting back to work, but most of the patients were used as "guinea pigs" in the name of science. When a patient died, it was no loss, as they would eventually all go to the gas chamber anyhow.

In one room, I saw large and small glass jars, each with some organ of the human body preserved in it. We were told that every part of the human body was there. Imagine! Innocent people dissected and displayed in these jars—their only crime being born a Jew!

In another room, we saw what appeared to be a painting on some type of parchment material. In reality this was a thin layer of skin taken from the backs of prisoners. These men were subjected to long sessions of tattooing until the whole back was covered with beautiful colors in many different patterns. When the picture was complete, the prisoner was injected with a death serum and the skin removed, then the body went to the crematory. These transparent paintings were used for lamp shades and back-lighted wall pictures. The German commander of this camp lived in a very nice home just outside the camp fence. We were not allowed in the house, but it was reported that his wife had many of these tattoos decorating the whole living area. Her specialty was lamp shades done to the liking of her warped mind. I believe she was tried and convicted in the post-war atrocity trials for her part in the revolting project.

In the rush to close the camp, the guards had started to kill off the inmates as quickly as possible. The gas chambers were used to their full capacity, but many prisoners were simply clubbed to death. We were taken to a building where prisoners were forced into a large room, all their clothes removed, then crowded into the next room. The door was shut and the gas turned on. The Final Solution!

The bodies were then burned in large ovens until only ashes remained. There was a large wagonload of corpses just outside, waiting for the furnaces. These were starved, emaciated, naked humans stacked high like cordwood. Each one had a dark purple bruise on the head where a club had caused his death.

Behind the crematory building were large piles of ashes from the ovens. Just outside the fence was a large field for growing cabbage. The prisoners had the unpleasant duty of spreading the ashes of their fellow prisoners on the cabbage field as fertilizer. The main diet had been cabbage soup with a lot of water and a little cabbage. Occasionally a little meat was added. One bowl of soup and one piece of black bread per day had been the regular ration.

Prophesy to the Land

To say that we were shocked as we left this terrible place would be an understatement. Here we were—young, healthy, strong, well-fed American soldiers—walking slowly, even reverently, around the horrors of this place with tears in our eyes. Such overpowering feelings of sympathy and sorrow for these people, none of us had ever experienced before.

Yes, we had seen many horrors of war. Cities and towns were bombed out of existence or young German soldiers were mowed down by American machine guns (having to bury them at times before we could set up our company in some field). I remember repairing Army trucks loaded high with frozen American bodies being taken from the front lines back to the undertaking units for identification and burial. None of these were pretty sights, but nothing had prepared us for what we had seen this day.

Not a word was spoken as we rode back to our camp area until someone asked how this could happen. How could anyone ever be so cruel? How could a nation sink so low as to allow this? Then someone asked why God had allowed this. Many more questions followed. All were valid questions with few real answers. We were told later that the following day, our troops went into the nearby town of Weimer and marched all the able-bodied townspeople to Camp Buchenwald to show them what was found there. They all pleaded innocent from any responsibility, claiming that they knew nothing about this place. With such a large operation, involving hundreds of military people and with all the trains bringing the prisoners there in boxcars, but with no prisoners ever leaving by train, somebody had to know something! I personally think that nobody really cared.

Tears

I recently watched a TV interview where two historical writers were asked if the atrocities of the Holocaust could ever be repeated. One answered no, that with modern technology these things could not be hidden from the world. The other gentleman, an elderly Jewish man, said yes, he believed it could happen again. He said it is not technology that would prevent it; rather these things happen because of the condition of men's hearts. He warned that only the condition of man's heart dictates how he feels about the value of life versus death. I felt a warning in his words, that we all need to put top priority on protecting the lives of all those who cannot speak for themselves.

It is estimated that in all of Europe, more than 12 million Jews died from all causes during the World War II period. It is a known fact that six million were deliberately killed in Hitler's death camps as "his solution to the Jewish problem."

The official account of Buchenwald says it was built as a labor camp in 1933. For several years, Jews were sent there for use as slave labor. Many died of disease, malnutrition, and overwork. However, it was not used as a death camp until later, after Hitler's army overran most of Europe. There were at this time six large death camps in Poland, where most of the Jews were sent to die. There were also 11 forced labor camps in Germany, including Buchenwald. As the war progressed, these also became death camps. There were also several death squads in the S.S. that moved all over Europe killing thousands, mostly Jews.

Buchenwald held about 20,000 prisoners at a time. It has been confirmed that more than 50,000 were killed there. It was the final destination for anyone, from all of occupied Europe, whose political views conflicted with Hitler's program. At the time of liberation on April 12, 1945, the inmates were described as the intelligentsia of Europe. Some of every nationality died in the gas chambers of Buchenwald, but it was mostly the Jews who were sent there for extermination. Hitler thought he had the "final solution to the Jewish problem." We know that only God has the solution to any problem and that Hitler's solution was doomed to failure because there was no place for God in his plans.

I don't know the answers to many of the questions about Buchenwald, but I do know what I saw on that April day in 1945. It was a terrible sight—a horrible reminder of the wickedness in the heart of man many years ago—before television. There was a mystery radio program that always went off the air with this question: "Who knows what evil lurks in the heart of man?" The answer has to be: God knows. I'm glad He has provided a way for man to exchange this natural evil for His goodness. My prayer in April of 1945 was, and still is, that places like Camp Buchenwald will never exist again.

—Lawrence Fuller, Clearwater, Florida

I appreciate my uncle's remembrance and would like to close this chapter with several pertinent quotations. After you read the following verses, also read the last chapters of Hosea and Joel. God will complete His plan to restore and bless Israel.

Thus says the Lord: "A voice was heard in Ramah, lamentation and bitter weeping, Rachel weeping for her children, refusing to be comforted for her children, because they are no more." Thus says the Lord: "Refrain your voice from weeping, and your eyes from tears; For your work shall be rewarded, says the Lord, and they shall come back from the land of the enemy. There is hope in your future, says the Lord, that your children shall come back to their own border" (Jeremiah 31:15-17).

Return, O backsliding children, says the Lord; "for I am married to you. I will take you, one from a city and two from a family, and I will bring you to Zion. ... In those days the house of Judah shall walk with the house of Israel, and they shall come together out of the land of the north to the land that I have given as an inheritance to your fathers" (Jeremiah 3:14,18).

Behold, I have refined you, but not as silver; I have tested you in the furnace of affliction (Isaiah 48:10).

For You, O God, have tested us; You have refined us as silver is refined. You brought us into the net; You laid affliction on our backs. You have caused men to ride over our heads; we went through fire and through water; but You brought us out to rich fulfillment (Psalm 66:10-12).

"On that day I will raise up the tabernacle of David, which has fallen down, and repair its damages; I will raise up its ruins, and rebuild it as in the days of old; that they may possess the remnant of Edom, and all the Gentiles who are called by My name," says the Lord who does this thing. "Behold, the days are coming," says the Lord, "When the plowman shall overtake the reaper, and the treader of grapes him who sows seed; the mountains shall drip with sweet wine, and all the hills shall flow with it. I will bring back the captives of My people Israel; They shall build the waste cities and inhabit them; they shall plant vineyards and drink wine

from them; they shall also make gardens and eat fruit from them. I will plant them in their land, and no longer shall they be pulled up from the land I have given them," says the Lord your God (Amos 9:11-15).

GOD IS FAITHFUL!

Chapter 16

Christ Killers!

The blame for killing Jesus has been such a central part of the persecution of the Jewish people for nearly 2,000 years that it is worth discussing the facts of the issue. There are actually three major errors of historical interpretation that have led to the hatred of the Jews and the widespread anti-Semitism that is directed their way. First, exactly who is responsible for Jesus' death? Second is the rejection error: Were the Jews eternally rejected? And third is the replacement error: Has Israel been replaced by the Church? The relationship between these three errors is similar to the classic domino effect. Start with the first, and the error deepens with each succeeding step.

The Responsibility Error

We begin by looking at the responsibility factor. There are three levels of culpability to consider: the physical, the psychological, and the spiritual. Before we can discuss who is responsible, we must first agree on the basic facts of His execution. Who put Him to death? The easy part is knowing who

Prophesy to the Land

hammered in the nails. It was the Roman soldiers under the command of Pontius Pilate who actually nailed Him to the cross. Though gruesome, this execution was a common form of capital punishment throughout the Roman Empire. It was the Romans' way of publicly intimidating their subjects into submission to the totalitarian rule of the Emperor of Rome. This method was also used on Christian martyrs in the years to follow. They were killed for such things as simply refusing to return the greeting: "Caesar is Lord!" Christians would respond by saying, "No, Jesus is Lord!" Jesus was crucified between two thieves by the Roman soldiers. "So the Scripture was fulfilled which says, 'And He was numbered with the transgressors' " (Mk. 15:28). Jesus was condemned by the Jewish religious court and by Pilate (representing Rome), in that he turned Jesus over to them in the first place.

This brings us to the second level of responsibility. On what basis could anyone say that Rome was not guilty of killing Jesus? They not only physically carried out the execution, they also directly considered the situation through Pilate and then made the legal decision to let the Jews do what they would with Him. John 19:10 says, "Then Pilate said to Him, 'Are You not speaking to me? Do You not know that I have power to crucify You, and power to release You?' " The Gentile rulers were very involved in the psychological aspect of the decision. This makes the Romans just as guilty as the Jews. In fact, this point is clearly confirmed in the Bible: "For truly against Your holy Servant Jesus, whom You anointed, both Herod and Pontius Pilate, with the Gentiles and the people of Israel, were gathered together to do whatever Your hand and Your purpose determined before to be done" (Acts 4:27-28). The Jews who were responsible had clearly stated their loyalty. "But they

Christ Killers!

cried out, 'Away with Him, away with Him! Crucify Him!' Pilate said to them, 'Shall I crucify your King?' The chief priests answered, 'We have no king but Caesar!' " (Jn. 19:15) Therefore we must conclude that both the Gentiles and the Jews are responsible, not the Jews *only*.

Now we come to the third level of responsibility. You and I are responsible for killing Jesus. He died because of you and me, because we have sinned. Jesus died for sinners—all sinners. He became God's perfect Lamb whose shed blood was acceptable to the supreme justice of the Father's character as the complete, total, once-and-for-all payment of sin. "By that will we have been sanctified through the offering of the body of Jesus Christ once for all. ... For by one offering He has perfected forever those who are being sanctified" (Heb. 10:10,14). This is applied to all who choose to repent and receive His Son Jesus. "But as many as received Him, to them He gave the right to become children of God, to those who believe in His name" (Jn. 1:12). There is another confirmation of this in Hebrews 6:4-6:

For it is impossible for those who were once enlightened, and have tasted the heavenly gift, and have become partakers of the Holy Spirit, and have tasted the good word of God and the powers of the age to come, if they fall away, to renew them again to repentance, since they crucify again for themselves the Son of God, and put Him to an open shame.

This indicates that our sin is what crucified Jesus. If we reject God's only plan of salvation, there is no way to be saved. There is no other plan; there is no plan B!

We have looked at all three levels of human responsibility, but we have not fully answered the question of who is responsible for killing Jesus. I would suggest a further consideration. God the Father and Jesus Himself are responsible! The Scriptures say of the Father in John 3:16, "For God so loved the world that He gave His only begotten Son, that whoever believes in Him should not perish but have everlasting life." God's love for us required that He give up the life of His Son. "He who did not spare His own Son, but delivered Him up for us all, how shall He not with Him also freely give us all things?" (Rom. 8:32). It is also true that Jesus Himself is responsible. "Therefore My Father loves Me, because I lay down My life that I may take it again. No one takes it from Me, but I lay it down of Myself. I have power to lay it down, and I have power to take it again. This command I have received from My Father" (Jn. 10:17-18). So we see that the answer to the first question of this chapter is that God the Father and the Son Himself share the responsibility for killing the Son.

The Rejection Error

Now that we know who killed Jesus and why, it becomes quite obvious that a grievous error was committed by theologians throughout church history. They have taught that God has rejected natural Israel *forever*. This error is still being repeated today and is the primary logical and philosophical basis for the anti-Semitism of history. (There is, of course, a satanic force that is responsible for the persecution in the spiritual dimension, one that has been at work trying to block God's plan of redemption from Cain on). In the human arena, since the Jews have been wrongly charged with the *responsibility* of Jesus' death, the cries of "Christ killers!" have fueled the emotions of countless thousands of persecutors and tormentors from the Hitlers to the average citizens.

Christ Killers!

The theological basis for this error states that since the Jews rejected Jesus by putting Him to death, God has therefore *rejected* them forever. God did reject those who refused Him and Israel was set aside for a season, but not forever. God has been known to cut off an entire generation: "So the Lord's anger was aroused against Israel, and He made them wander in the wilderness forty years, until all the generation that had done evil in the sight of the Lord was gone" (Num. 32:13). But the wandering Diaspora (or dispersion) after they rejected Jesus makes the judgment of Moses' day seem light by comparison. Now, I am not disputing the judgment of God; I am simply pointing out that there is a promised return to mercy for the Jews and the land of Israel. Jeremiah 31:35-37 makes an amazing point:

> *Thus says the Lord, who gives the sun for a light by day, the ordinances of the moon and the stars for a light by night, who disturbs the sea, and its waves roar (The Lord of hosts is His name): "If those ordinances depart from before Me, says the Lord, then the seed of Israel shall also cease from being a nation before Me forever." Thus says the Lord: "If heaven above can be measured, and the foundations of the earth searched out beneath, I will also cast off all the seed of Israel for all that they have done, says the Lord."*

God declares that Israel will always be a nation before Him. This is not a "spiritual nation," but a physical one; a nation in the time-space context of this age of the physical sun, moon, and stars.

Paul teaches in Romans, chapters 9 through 11 about the issue of Israel's future status. One key verse is Romans 11:23:

"And they also, if they do not continue in unbelief, will be grafted in, for God is able to graft them in again." He then goes on to state the bottom-line basis for their restoration in verses 26-29:

And so all Israel will be saved, as it is written: "The Deliverer will come out of Zion, and He will turn away ungodliness from Jacob; for this is My covenant with them, when I take away their sins." Concerning the gospel they are enemies for your sake, but concerning the election they are beloved for the sake of the fathers. For the gifts and the calling of God are irrevocable (Romans 11:26-29).

This tremendous principle is the theme of my entire book: *God will not revoke His callings*! God is faithful to His word. Notice it says that they are enemies concerning the gospel, but "*concerning the election*" God loves them! Natural Israel is part of the elect of God. He loves them not according to their behavior, whether sinful or not, but for their forefathers' sake. It is based on a verse that most of us have claimed personally at some time or another. But in order to apply it to ourselves, we must spiritualize it. The actual, *literal* context of verse 29 is nothing less than the restoration of natural Israel. God does not take back His gifts or His callings once He has spoken. God had given that spoken word to Abraham, Isaac, and Jacob. He will not revoke it. Israel's rejection was for a temporary purpose, even though that time lasted 1,900 years. Their grafting back in is ensured, not by any event of history or action of Israel, but by the unchangeable character of God's faithfulness.

Let us take a brief look at church history and see some of the official roots of this error.

Christ Killers!

Around A.D. 306, church leaders meeting in Elvira, Spain, issued a decree forbidding close relations of any kind between Christians and Jews. In particular they banned Jewish/Christian marriages, which was understandable in light of Paul's admonition in his second letter to the Corinthians that Christians should not be "unequally yoked" with nonbelievers (6:14).

The Nicaean Council of 325 took another step to insure that Christians would have "nothing in common with this odious people," ruling that the calendar date for Easter should be unlinked to the Jewish Passover Festival. The Council of Antioch in 341 explicitly prohibited Christians from celebrating Passover with their Jewish neighbors (a command I've broken many times!). The long running Council of Laodicea (434-481) told Christians they could not keep the Jewish Sabbath, or receive gifts or unleavened bread from Jews observing the Passover.

The Roman Emperor Constantine converted to Christianity in 312 and later declared his new faith to be the official state religion. His subsequent moves regarding the Jewish people were not exactly sterling displays of the Golden Rule. Constantine ordered all Jews to leave Rome in 325, signaling hard times ahead for the ancient chosen people of God. British Old Testament scholar H.L. Ellis wrote that Constantine's legalization of Christianity was a turning point for the Jews: "When the church became recognized by Constantine, legal discrimination against Jews increased and they were gradually deprived of all rights."(1)

These legal changes continued over the centuries and are well documented.

> The expulsion of the Jews from Spain and Portugal followed what was probably the saddest feature of Roman Catholic church history: the Inquisition. Pope Sixtus IV issued a Papal Bull in 1478 to set up the "Holy Tribunal" in Spain. Its purpose was to seek out and expose all heretics living in the land. The Roman Catholic Inquisitors ordered tens of thousands of people burned alive at the stake, most of them either Jews who had been pressured to convert to Christianity or their descendants. Many confessed, often under torture, that they had clung to Judaism despite their conversions. ... The Reformation was in fact welcomed by many Jews as a possible breath of fresh air in an otherwise stifling Europe. Martin Luther had proclaimed that Christians must be guided in their dealings with the Jews, "not by papal law, but by the law of Christian love." Yet a mere twenty years later, Luther—upset that "Christian love" had not won mass conversions—declared the Jews "disgusting vermin" who should be deported from Germany. His pamphlet "On The Jews and Their Lies" (1543) called for seven steps to be taken against the Jews, including the burning of their synagogues, the razing of their houses, the banning of their holy books, and the seizure of their assets.(2)

It is also fact of history that Hitler used quotes from Luther as part of his justification for the Holocaust.

The age-old justification for this unchristlike treatment of His chosen people was their error that God had "permanently" rejected the Jews for their rejection of Jesus. However, this was not the end of the downward spiral. They further developed the doctrine of what would come to be known as "replacement theology."

Christ Killers!

The Replacement Error

Having made the first two errors (of responsibility and rejection), it was a logical step to declare the church to be the new Israel. Since all those unfulfilled promises of God for Israel were still there (and with the Jews disposed of by tidy theological manipulations), the Church must be God's replacement of the rejected Jews, thus becoming the new Israel! The system was now complete. No longer did they have to bother with all those literal interpretations; now they could spiritualize to their hearts' content. What those theologians had not counted on, however, was the God of history's intervention and imposition into their plans. With every literal fulfillment of ancient prophecies in our day, their theories are further exposed and undermined.

The theological problem for proponents of the replacement theory is their ending up with God having two wives, or God the Father with an ex-wife and Jesus with a wife. Atlanta pastor Earl Paulk has written a book entitled *To Whom Is God Betrothed?* that seeks to explain this particular subject, but that makes many errors. The first is in his Introduction: "The Bible is a story of covenant, a marriage relationship between God and mankind. One covenant failed because of continuous disobedience."(3) The key word here is *failed*. I do not agree. The Old Testament did not fail; it did exactly what it was supposed to do. It taught man that he could never fulfill the law and that he needed the Messiah: "Therefore the law was our tutor to bring us to Christ, that we might be justified by faith" (Gal. 3:24). No one was ever saved by keeping the law, but by believing in the Messiah whom God had promised. That was as true for the Old Testament saints as it is for us! That doesn't indicate failure of the first covenant! It did exactly what it was supposed to do; it turned men to *Christ*, which is the Greek word for *Messiah*. The difference is that now we know His name is Jesus, and the sacrifice is completed. Righteousness was always accounted on the basis of faith.

Earl Paulk also takes issue with the Book of Hosea:

In the book of Hosea, we find in-depth understanding of Israel's infidelity toward God. Israel is referred to as the Lord's "wife," but the prophet Hosea upbraided Israel because she became a harlot against Jehovah God. Israel intermarried and practiced pagan religions. Again and again God tried to bring Israel back into the marriage relationship with Him. Finally God said, "It is hopeless! I have been married to a harlot and a backslider. Now I must break the covenant with her." Israel is referred to as the Lord's "wife," whereas the Church is called "the Bride of Christ."(4)

Does the Book of Hosea in your Bible say that? My Bible differs in the following ways: (a) Gomer was already a harlot when Hosea married her. (b) God certainly does *not* finally say, "It is hopeless." I could never imagine those words from the mouth of the Almighty. In fact, He says the opposite:

Therefore, behold, I will allure her, will bring her into the wilderness, and speak comfort to her. I will give her her vineyards from there, and the Valley of Achor as a door of hope; she shall sing there, as in the days of her youth, as in the day when she came up from the land of Egypt (Hosea 2:14-15).

He speaks of a "door of hope." (c) God never says such a thing as "I will break covenant with her." In fact, I believe that to suggest that God is a covenant breaker is blasphemy. This is what God actually says in Hosea 2:19-20: "I will betroth you to Me forever; yes, I will betroth you to Me in righteousness and justice, in lovingkindness and mercy; I will betroth you to Me in faithfulness, and you shall know the Lord." He uses the words *forever* and *faithfulness* as the action He will take to betroth her. He then adds in Hosea 3:4-5:

For the children of Israel shall abide many days without king or prince, without sacrifice or sacred pillar, without ephod or teraphim. Afterward the children of Israel shall return and seek the Lord their God and David their king. They shall fear the Lord and His goodness in the latter days.

If this is not a description of the last 1,900 years, I don't know what is. It is as though Rev. Paulk did not read the end of the book! The very book of the Bible he quotes to try and prove that God has replaced Israel, actually proves that God will restore Israel!

I will heal their backsliding, I will love them freely, for My anger has turned away from him. I will be like the dew to Israel; he shall grow like the lily, and lengthen his roots like Lebanon. His branches shall spread; his beauty shall be like an olive tree, and his fragrance like Lebanon. Those who dwell under his shadow shall return; they shall be revived like grain, and grow like a vine. Their scent shall be like the wine of Lebanon (Hosea 14:4-7).

If you are interested in studying more about replacement theology, I recommend Keith Parker's pamphlet "Is the Church the New Israel."(5)

Let me close this chapter on a personal note. In January, 1990, I attended the International Intercessors Prayer Conference in Jerusalem sponsored by Steve Lightle and Exodus II Ministries. Steve wrote an excellent book entitled *Exodus II* that you should certainly read if possible.(6) At the end of the conference we were in Tiberias worshiping with a Messianic believers' fellowship of some 300 people at a love feast dinner held in a hotel. I sat around the table with Israeli Jewish believers from America, Israel, England, Iraq, Iran, and Siberia! It was after dinner that I hugged the neck of that Russian Jewish Pentecostal pastor who had just recently won his citizenship in Israel.

For thus says the Lord: "Sing with gladness for Jacob, and shout among the chief of the nations; proclaim, give praise, and say, 'O Lord, save Your people, the remnant of Israel!' Behold, I will bring them from the north country, and gather them from the ends of the earth, among them the blind and the lame, the woman with child and the one who labors with child, together; a great throng shall return there. They shall come with weeping, and with supplications I will lead them. I will cause them to walk by the rivers of waters, in a straight way in which they shall not stumble; for I am a Father to Israel, and Ephraim is My firstborn" (Jeremiah 31:7-9).

I am thankful to be alive in this great and glorious day of Israel's restoration and return!

GOD IS FAITHFUL!

Chapter 17

I Will Kibbutz You

The twentieth century will be remembered for the many amazing events that made history, including the world wars, the rise and fall of Marxist Communism, space exploration (especially putting man on the moon), and explosions of information, population, technology, and humanism. Yet, from the wider perspective of 6,000 years of human history, the most significant story of this century may well be the regathering of God's people from the four corners of the earth, including most astoundingly, from Russia and her allies, the "Pharaoh of the North."

"Hear the word of the Lord, O nations, and declare it in the isles afar off, and say, 'He who scattered Israel will gather him, and keep him as a shepherd does his flock' " (Jer. 31:10). It is from this verse that I obtain the name for this chapter. Just as surely as it was God who scattered Israel, it is God who will regather them and bring them back to the land. An amazing and little known fact is hidden in the original Hebrew language of this verse. The word for *gather* in Hebrew is *kibbutz*. That word should sound familiar to you because it is also used in English as the name of the communal settlements in Israel that were one of the grandest and most successful social experiments of the twentieth Century. I quote from Dr. Derek Prince, a prominent Hebrew and Greek language scholar.

> Let me point out another interesting fact that confirms in an amazing way the absolute accuracy of biblical prophecy. The Hebrew word used here for "gathering" comes from a basic verb form: *kibbetz*. The same basic form also gives us the modern Hebrew word *kibbutz* (of which the plural is *kibbutzim*).
>
> A *kibbutz* may be defined roughly as a group of people who settle together on an area of land, pool their resources and lead a communal kind of life. The original emphasis of nearly all *kibbutzim* in Israel was primarily agricultural, although today there have been other developments. It is an objective fact of history that the *kibbutzim* have played a unique and vital part in the growth of modern Israel. They have made an indispensable contribution to both the economy and the defense of the state.(1)

In the regathering after the Babylonian captivity, Nehemiah appeals to God's faithful word as he seeks the Lord's blessing on the rebuilding of the walls of Jerusalem in 444 B.C.

> *Remember, I pray, the word that You commanded Your servant Moses, saying, "If you are unfaithful, I will scatter you among the nations; but if you return to Me, and keep My commandments and do them, though some of you were cast out to the farthest part of the heavens, yet I will gather them from there, and bring them to the place which I have chosen as a dwelling for My name"* (Nehemiah 1:8-9).

I Will Kibbutz You

The basis for the Jewish hope of restoration is on the mercy and faithfulness of God. Yet this restoration will not be without suffering and trouble. Neither will it contradict God's justice; He continues to correct Israel (and us) through tribulation and trouble.

Jacob's Trouble

The following passage includes the reference often quoted by prophetic Bible teachers regarding "Jacob's trouble." This is usually placed during the "Great Tribulation" of prophecy, but I would suggest that it sounds a lot like the Holocaust. I don't think I would like to tell a Holocaust survivor that his experience was not great tribulation! If the annihilation of six million Jews is not trouble for Jacob, I can't imagine worse. Perhaps this "Jacob's trouble" is not the tribulation that is still to come. After Jesus comes back, we will all see clearly with that wonderful 20-20 hindsight. But for now, just consider the precision of this part of Jeremiah's prophecy that we can see is already fulfilled.

> *" 'For behold, the days are coming,' says the Lord, 'that I will bring back from captivity My people Israel and Judah,' says the Lord. 'And I will cause them to return to the land that I gave to their fathers, and they shall possess it.' " Now these are the words that the Lord spoke concerning Israel and Judah. "For thus says the Lord: 'We have heard a voice of trembling, of fear, and not of peace. Ask now, and see, whether a man is ever in labor with child? So why do I see every man with his hands on his loins like a woman in labor, and all faces turned pale? Alas! For that day is great, So that none is like it; and it is the time of Jacob's trouble, but he shall*

> *be saved out of it. For it shall come to pass in that day,' says the Lord of hosts, 'that I will break his yoke from your neck, and will burst your bonds; foreigners shall no more enslave them. But they shall serve the Lord their God, and David their king, whom I will raise up for them. Therefore do not fear, O My servant Jacob,' says the Lord, 'nor be dismayed, O Israel; for behold, I will save you from afar, and your seed from the land of their captivity. Jacob shall return, have rest and be quiet, and no one shall make him afraid. For I am with you,' says the Lord, 'to save you; though I make a full end of all nations where I have scattered you, yet I will not make a complete end of you. But I will correct you in justice, and will not let you go altogether unpunished' "* (Jeremiah 30:3-11).

There is an interesting comment at the end of this passage. God suggests that He will "make a full end" of all the other nations, but will not end Israel. Yet there are some today who insist that God is through with Israel. It is a fact of history that every civilization that falls never comes back. Yet just the opposite is true of Israel. God will bring correction and punishment, but Israel will survive!

The Set Time to Favor Zion

> *You will arise and have mercy on Zion; for the time to favor her, yes, the set time, has come. ... For the Lord shall build up Zion; He shall appear in His glory. He shall regard the prayer of the destitute, and shall not despise their prayer. This will be written for the generation to come, that a people yet to be created may praise the Lord. For He looked down from the height of His*

sanctuary; from heaven the Lord viewed the earth, to hear the groaning of the prisoner, to release those appointed to death, to declare the name of the Lord in Zion, and His praise in Jerusalem, when the peoples are gathered together, and the kingdoms, to serve the Lord (Psalm 102:13,16-22).

The Lord heard the groaning of the prisoner, and that triggered something in God's timing that allowed Him to release them for restoration in the set time! That is why we can now proclaim comfort to Zion—that her sins are forgiven (through Jesus) and that she has paid double for all her sins. We must proclaim the prophetic message of Isaiah 40:1-2: " 'Comfort, yes, comfort My people!' says your God. 'Speak comfort to Jerusalem, and cry out to her, that her warfare is ended, that her iniquity is pardoned; for she has received from the Lord's hand double for all her sins.' "

Fishers and Hunters

How does God bring His people back? Is there some heavenly signal like a beautiful trumpet sounding the return? I'm afraid not. However, the Bible is not silent about this part of the plan. With great precision the Scriptures reveal exactly how God will do it. "I will bring the blind by a way they did not know; I will lead them in paths they have not known. I will make darkness light before them, and crooked places straight. These things I will do for them, and not forsake them" (Is. 42:16). Another clear statement of their blindness in found in Isaiah 29:9-11:

Pause and wonder! Blind yourselves and be blind! They are drunk, but not with wine; they stagger, but not with intoxicating drink. For the Lord has poured out on you

> the spirit of deep sleep, and has closed your eyes, namely, the prophets; and He has covered your heads, namely, the seers. The whole vision has become to you like the words of a book that is sealed, which men deliver to one who is literate, saying, "Read this, please." And he says, "I cannot, for it is sealed."

The fact that they are still blind at this point agrees with the other passages we have been considering (see also Rom. 11:8-10).

Because they are blinded, God will send what the Bible calls fishers and hunters to bring them back to the land.

> But, "The Lord lives who brought up the children of Israel from the land of the north and from all the lands where He had driven them." For I will bring them back into their land which I gave to their fathers. "Behold, I will send for many fishermen," says the Lord, "and they shall fish them; and afterward I will send for many hunters, and they shall hunt them from every mountain and every hill, and out of the holes of the rocks" (Jeremiah 16:15-16).

This passage in Jeremiah is the basis for an excellent book called *Fishers and Hunters* by Meridel Rawlings, and I quote from her Preface:

> Over 2,500 years ago the prophets of Israel forecast the ingathering of the Jews and the rebuilding of their nation in the Land of Israel. Today living in Israel are 3½ million Jews from over 100 nations of the world. By this immigration, particularly during the last 60 years, we know the Holy Spirit is doing this work as promised. Israel as a modern nation was born after the tragic loss of six million

Jews in the death camps of the Nazi Holocaust. Perhaps Jeremiah foresaw this...worldwide terrorist activity and referred to them as "hunters"?

"I will send for many fishers..." is the other portion of that prophetic word. Fishermen are quiet and gentle; in this case their desire is to catch the "fish" and see them transferred from the great rivers of the world, so to speak, back to their spawning ground where they belong—Israel.(2)

First the fishers, then the hunters; can there be any doubt that we are seeing this process with our own eyes in this generation? If the fishers are now at work in the United States, can the hunters be far behind? I hope such a tragic scenario does not happen here, but I do know one thing. There are 8.5 million Jews residing in comfort in North and South America whom God is calling back to their roots in the Holy Land of Israel. By the way, since Meridel Rawlings wrote her book in 1982, more than one million more Jews have returned, bringing the total to nearly five million in the land!

The Greater Exodus

The Russians are coming! The Russians are coming! Moses led the children of Israel out of the slavery of Egypt in what became the single most remembered and quoted event in the history of Israel. Jewish families continue to observe the great "passing over" of the death angel every year at the biblical feast bearing the name of that great event: Passover. They recite repeatedly the great deliverance from Egypt. Yet there is a prophetic promise to Israel in the Book of Jeremiah that, when considered in context, is nothing less than mind-boggling. It is in the verse just preceding the one we read about the fishers and hunters:

Therefore behold, the days are coming," says the Lord, "that it shall no more be said, 'The Lord lives who brought up the children of Israel from the land of Egypt,' but, 'The Lord lives who brought up the children of Israel from the land of the north and from all the lands where He had driven them.' For I will bring them back into their land which I gave to their fathers" (Jeremiah 16:14-15; also see Jeremiah 23:3-8).

What kind of incredible exodus from the north must take place to actually supplant the traditional Jewish ritual prayers remembering Egypt? Notice it says, "from the land of the north *and from all the lands*" (emphasis mine). This phenomenal return includes all of North and South America. How will it happen? When will it happen? I don't know, but it will happen, and it will be soon!

We should make sure our prayers are in agreement with God and join in prophesying with Ezekiel, Jeremiah, Isaiah, Zechariah and all the prophets, ancient and contemporary.

Fear not, for I am with you; I will bring your descendants from the east, and gather you from the west; I will say to the north, "Give them up!" And to the south, "Do not keep them back!" Bring My sons from afar, and My daughters from the ends of the earth (Isaiah 43:5-6).

For some years now, many intercessors have been directly praying against the "Pharaoh of the North" to "Give them up!" As recently as late 1989, this quote was still being seen as symbolic by many scholars. Russian Jews were only allowed to leave in a trickle. But with the unprecedented changes in the former U.S.S.R. and throughout Eastern Europe, we are seeing the literal fulfillment of this Scripture in the 1990's. The fall of the U.S.S.R. has been astounding, but the result is nearly half a million Russian Jews who have already come to Israel in the last two years, and over a million who are waiting to come with exit visas already in their hands. Proclaim the Word of the Lord:

Yet hear now, O Jacob My servant, and Israel whom I have chosen. Thus says the Lord who made you and formed you from the womb, who will help you: "Fear not, O Jacob My servant; and you, Jeshurun, whom I have chosen. For I will pour water on him who is thirsty, and floods on the dry ground; I will pour My Spirit on your descendants, and My blessing on your offspring; they will spring up among the grass like willows by the watercourses." One will say, "I am the Lord's"; another will call himself by the name of Jacob; another will write with his hand, "The Lord's," and name himself by the name of Israel. Thus says the Lord, the King of Israel, and his Redeemer, the Lord of hosts: "I am the First and I am the Last; besides Me there is no God. And who can proclaim as I do? Then let him declare it and set it in order for Me, since I appointed the ancient people. And the things that are coming and shall come, let them show these to them. Do not fear, nor be afraid; have I not told you from that time, and declared it? You are My witnesses. Is there a God besides Me? Indeed there is no other Rock; I know not one" (Isaiah 44:1-8).

There is so much said about this final regathering that we should be in awe.

Behold, I will bring them from the north country, and gather them from the ends of the earth, among them the blind and the lame, the woman with child and the one who labors with child, together; a great throng shall return there. They shall come with weeping, and with supplications I will lead them. I will cause them to walk by the rivers of waters, in a straight way in which they shall not stumble; for I am a Father to Israel, and Ephraim is My firstborn. Hear the word of the Lord, O nations, and declare it in the isles afar off, and say, "He who scattered Israel will gather him, and keep him as a shepherd does his flock" (Jeremiah 31:8-10).

I need to comment on one other point concerning a common objection to this doctrine of the return in this century. Some Bible teachers claim that the phrase "the second time" in Isaiah 11:11 refers to the Babylonian captivity: "It shall come to pass in that day that the Lord shall set His hand again the second time to recover the remnant of His people who are left, from Assyria and Egypt, from Pathros and Cush, from Elam and Shinar, from Hamath and the islands of the sea." There are two clear errors in trying to apply this verse to any other return before now. First, the Babylonian captivity was only in one country, certainly not the lengthy list in the verse. Second, the context of Isaiah 11 is clearly about Jesus' first coming. The recovery of the remnant clearly *follows* Jesus being exalted *and* the Gentiles' seeking Him. This is in complete agreement with our understanding of the time of the Gentiles, as we will see in Chapter 20. This same order is repeated in the next verse: "He will set up a banner for the nations, and will assemble the outcasts of Israel, and gather together the dispersed of Judah from the four corners of the earth" (Is. 11:12). There is still another indication of a future return that could not refer to Babylon. "And they shall rebuild the old ruins, they shall raise up the former desolations, and they shall repair the ruined cities, the desolations of many generations" (Is. 61:4). The Babylonian exile lasted only 70 years, one or two generations at the most. But Isaiah saw a rebuilding that would repair the desolations of "many generations." The precision of God's prophetic Scriptures and their fulfillment is a marvelous wonder to behold.

GOD IS FAITHFUL!

Chapter 18

Israel at the End of the Twentieth Century

Can a Nation Be born in a Day? On November 29, 1947, the United Nations voted to allow the establishment of a national homeland for the Jewish people in a portion of the area in the Middle East known throughout history as the Holy Land. This change was to be effective at the official withdrawal of all British troops. The last troops left, the Israel Declaration of Independence was signed, and the state of Israel was proclaimed at 4 p.m. on May 14, 1948. Thus was fulfilled one of the more precise prophetic verses in the Bible: "Who has heard such a thing? Who has seen such things? Shall the earth be made to give birth in one day? Or shall a nation be born at once? For as soon as Zion was in labor, she gave birth to her children" (Is. 66:8).

Derek Prince, who was living in Jerusalem on that momentous day, made this comment:

> That was exactly what I had been permitted to see with my own eyes! On one day—May 14, 1948—Israel was born as a complete nation, with its own government, armed forces and all necessary administrative functions. True, everything had been improvised hastily and on a small scale. Yet all the necessary ingredients were there to make Israel a sovereign nation within its own borders. So far as I knew, such an event was without parallel in human history.(1)

Almost overnight the land began to prosper and blossom with trees, flowers, and people! There was literally dancing in the streets that was recorded and broadcast around the world. "And the ransomed of the Lord shall return, and come to Zion with singing, with everlasting joy on their heads. They shall obtain joy and gladness, and sorrow and sighing shall flee away" (Is. 35:10). God was beginning to fulfill His ancient covenant word to this pivotal generation. As I mentioned earlier, many Jews had already been returning, for 50 years before that day. Kibbutzim had been established; the great Jezreel valley swamps had been drained and irrigated and were ready to furnish the food needed to feed this new nation. As God prospered them, He was keeping His word to their fathers.

Desert Flowers

One great prophecy is the one about the desert blossoming: "The wilderness and the wasteland shall be glad for them, and the desert shall rejoice and blossom as the rose" (Is.35:1). There are still those who argue that this is not fulfilled prophecy because it was accomplished with human means, such as irrigation and hard physical work. I have two comments to make about that objection. First, where is it written that God does not use man to fulfill His word? When Jesus had His disciples get a donkey for the "triumphal entry" into Jerusalem, prophecy was fulfilled. When the angry mob chose Barabbas instead of Jesus, prophecy was fulfilled. Isaiah 53:12 declares, "Therefore I will divide Him a portion with the great, and He shall divide the spoil with the strong, because He poured out His soul unto death, and He was numbered with the transgressors, and He bore the sin of many, and made intercession for the transgressors." So we see that God freely uses people to bring His word to pass.

I have a second reason for why the desert rose prophecy is being fulfilled. In addition to the efforts of the Israelis, there is a phenomenon taking place that is nothing short of supernatural—I have seen it with my own eyes. Each time I go to Israel, there is more "green." When I first traveled there with my wife Doreen in 1984, Israel was in a severe drought. As a result, we were inspired to begin to pray for rain, along with many other intercessors. We asked on the basis of Joel 2:23: "Be glad then, you children of Zion, and rejoice in the Lord your God; for He has given you the former rain faithfully, and He will cause the rain to come down for you; The former rain, and the latter rain in the first month."

Now you may say that Joel's prophecy concerned the Holy Spirit, as quoted by the apostle Peter in Acts 2, and you are right. I believe with all my heart that we are living in the latter rain of the Holy Spirit and that this rain is indeed greater than the former rain at Pentecost and the first century. But in accepting only this position, what happens to Zechariah 10:1? "Ask the Lord for rain in the time of the latter rain. The Lord will make flashing clouds; He will give them showers of rain, grass in the field for everyone." I believe this verse combines the

Prophesy to the Land

spiritual promise and the literal physical promise of rain during that season. Flashing clouds, showers, and grass sound pretty literal to me. (As I have stated before, I believe we should always see the literal interpretation if at all possible). The only prerequisite is that we "*ask the Lord for rain.*"

"I have set watchmen on your walls, O Jerusalem; they shall never hold their peace day or night. You who make mention of the Lord, do not keep silent, and give Him no rest till He establishes and till He makes Jerusalem a praise in the earth" (Is. 62:6-7). Many faithful intercessors prayed for rain in the dry time of the 1980's (which was spiritually dry for many as well), and God has begun to bring back the rains to the land! Unprecedented snow (a foot in Jerusalem), rain, and other forms of precipitation have blessed the land in 1991 and 1992. All-time records have fallen. It is a well-known fact that the deserts of Israel are composed of the most fertile soil on earth, which is filled with dormant seeds waiting to spring to life. All you need to do is add water! God and the Israeli people are doing that at a record pace. So keep praying and asking.

A fascinating fact was told to us by our guide on one of our trips to Israel. When I came home I checked out a few facts with my father-in-law who had been a farmer in Maine. He said farmers there could get one-and-a-half cuttings of hay per year, and in a really good year, maybe two cuttings. I also discovered that in Georgia farmers can get three cuttings of hay. The fact that astounds me about the fertility of Israeli soil is that the Hulah Valley near the Sea of Galilee has had as many as 18 cuttings of hay in one year! God loves the land of Israel and delights in providing abundantly.

Therefore they shall come and sing in the height of Zion, streaming to the goodness of the Lord—for wheat and

> *new wine and oil, for the young of the flock and the herd; their souls shall be like a well-watered garden, and they shall sorrow no more at all. Then shall the virgin rejoice in the dance, and the young men and the old, together; for I will turn their mourning to joy, will comfort them, and make them rejoice rather than sorrow. I will satiate the soul of the priests with abundance, and My people shall be satisfied with My goodness, says the Lord* (Jeremiah 31:12-14).

Jesus also declared this in John 10:10: "The thief does not come except to steal, and to kill, and to destroy. I have come that they may have life, and that they may have it more abundantly."

The Sabra

There is an interesting little cactus that grows and flowers in the deserts of Israel called a sabra. It is known for its rugged tenaciousness. It will grow under the most adverse conditions and is almost impossible to kill. What makes it even more interesting is that its name has been borrowed in modern Hebrew vernacular to be the name for native-born Israelis. Naturally a large part of the population has always been comprised of the many immigrants who have made *aliya*. (*Aliya* is the Hebrew word for "going up," which is used to describe immigration to Zion. Once they are transplanted they are called *olim*). Yet as the population booms, more and more are being *born* in the land. What makes this significant is these sabras are somewhat different from their fathers who have returned from the Diaspora (scattering). Those returning usually had been "taught their place" and were often the victims of extreme persecution and all forms of anti-Semitism. There was a sort of

Prophesy to the Land

"victim" mentality that settled in on many of the persecuted ones. Consider the wonder of the many Jews who had submissively yielded to the Nazis herding them like cattle onto the boxcars and taking them to the gas chambers. But the Israeli-born sabras were born free men in every way! They have a distinct outlook on the world that takes into account the atrocities committed against their ancestors, but with a new boldness and resolve that says, "Never again!"

Our guide, on our first trip to Israel in 1984, thrilled our group with a true story he told us while he stood on Masada with his back to the Roman ramp. That earthen ramp represented the end of the stand-off that had lasted nearly three years after the fall of Jerusalem in A.D. 70. The holdout was successful because of the remote location of Masada, the flat-topped mountain with sheer cliffs overlooking the Dead Sea. The whole story of the Jews' stubborn survival to the end was inspiring (so much so, in fact, that it was made into a movie). But the highlight of our trip was when our guide, Moshe, with the wind blowing his hair, had us look to the horizon for 360 degrees. He pointed out that today, the baby nation of Israel is surrounded on all sides by hostile Arab nations just like the Romans had gathered their troops around Masada, having sworn to drive Israel into the sea. But this time Israel is saying, "Never again!" It is even the slogan of one of their elite fighting units who have their commissioning ceremonies on Masada. God's will is going to win out no matter what the human odds. You, plus God, are always enough to win any battle.

The Dead Language

What many people do not realize is the Hebrew language was just as dead as Latin. It was used sparingly in Jewish religious circles, but not nearly as much in comparison to Latin. Latin is used not only in the Roman Catholic Church, but also for legal and scientific jargon. Hebrew was not spoken by any people as their native language for nearly 2,000 years. The language spoken in many Jewish homes was either Yiddish, a mixture of German and Hebrew, or Ladino, a mixture of old Spanish, Arabic, and Hebrew.

Yet God has precisely foretold by the prophets that He would restore Hebrew! "Thus says the Lord of hosts, the God of Israel: 'They shall again use this speech in the land of Judah and in its cities, when I bring back their captivity: "The Lord bless you, O home of justice, and mountain of holiness!" ' " (Jer. 31:23) It is also suggested in Zephaniah 3:9, "For then I will restore to the peoples a pure language, that they all may call on the name of the Lord, to serve Him with one accord." It is amazing to realize that Israelis today come from more than 100 different nations of the earth with nearly as many languages, and yet they all learn Hebrew. One of the obligations for every returning Jew is a 4½ month "ulpan" which is an intensive all day, six days a week Hebrew language study.

I highly recommend the excellent book *Tongue of the Prophets*, the biography of Eliezer Ben Yehuda, the father of modern Hebrew. It is the story of the rebirth of the Hebrew language, written by Robert St. John.(2) It tells of his children being the first children in millennia to learn Hebrew as their mother tongue, and traces the process that has led to Hebrew being the functional and official language of Israel. This is nothing short of miraculous: a language raised from the dead!

The State of Palestine?

If you were asked to name all the periods of history that had an independent self-governing state of Palestine, how many could you name? How long is the list? I must admit that this is a trick question. There have been *none*! This may come as a surprise to you, in light of the pleas from Palestinians through the media for the right to return to "their" land. There has never been an independent Palestinian state.

According the Christian Friends of Israel publication *Zion Quarterly*:

> Both Jews and Arabs have deep roots in the land of Israel. Jewish roots go back at least 3,700 years to Abraham, who God called out of Ur of the Chaldees to dwell in the land of Canaan. Jewish national history on the land begins with Joshua in about 1240 B.C., comes to its zenith with the kingdoms of David and Solomon, and continues until the dispersion in 70 A.D. Throughout the nearly 2000 years of exile, Jews have continued to pray and long for the restoration of Jewish sovereignty and a national home in the Promised Land.
>
> The exact origin of the Arabs in Palestine is less clear. In the sense that the word "Arab" means nomads or Bedouin tribes, Arabs have lived on the land for thousands of years. But in its original sense, the word "Arab" refers to the tribes of the Arabian desert; and it was not until the Moslem-Arab conquest of Palestine in the 7th Century A.D. that the Bedouin tribes of Palestine actually became "Arabized"— that is, adopting the Arabic language and culture.
>
> But while the Arabs have dwelt in the land in one form or another for centuries, they were never, until recently, called Palestinians; they were never separate from the entire Arab nation, and there has never been an independent Arab state in this land called Palestine.(3)

Israel at the End of the Twentieth Century

I personally find it ironic that there is so much confusion about this subject. It was the Romans who changed the name from Judea to Palestine sometime after the fall of Jerusalem in A.D. 70, in an attempt to remove the memory of the Jews' ownership. It was pretty successful, I might add. Even our Bible maps have plastered the name Palestine all over them, even those of Jesus' time. But the Bible does not record Jesus being born in Bethlehem of Palestine, but in Bethlehem of Judea! How much has the propaganda affected all of us? How many of the 75 New Testament references (New King James version) are speaking of literal Israel and how many are speaking of spiritual Israel? Would you believe only one refers to spiritual Israel? That is Galations 6:16. Count them for yourself. Selah. Think about it.

"David Loses to Goliath!"

There is a propaganda war being won by the Palestinians. They are trying to rewrite history and have Goliath win. There are no prophecies or promises to the Palestinians, other than those of salvation and blessing to all who receive Jesus as Messiah and Lord. They enjoy no "land covenant" promises. If they did, I would be for their biblical fulfillment just as much as for Israel's. I am not so much pro-Israel as I am pro-God.

Amazingly, no groups were called Palestinians over the years, and ironically, it was the returning Jews who were called Palestinians as they dwelt in the land. This was simply because the British had picked up the old Roman designation. It was only after the Jewish people became a nation on May 14, 1948, and took the name Israel (being split closely between Israel and Judea in their vote), that the Arabs started using the term for their own ends. It was because of the association it had in the minds of Westerners that the name *Palestinians* had some real political value for the Arabs. It was a brilliant choice because they not only had instant identity, but more importantly, they had instant sympathy. By seizing on the refugee problem (augmented by their refusal to absorb their own people in Jordan, Syria, and Egypt) they had an "issue" that would serve them well in the years to come (from 1948 to the present).

With this and other moves, such as getting children to throw rocks at soldiers (which became the Intifada), they managed to re-cast the roles of David and Goliath! Even though they outnumbered Israel 120 million to 3 million at the time, they succeeded in molding world opinion to believe that little "Israel Goliath" was beating up on the entire Arab nation's "David." This continues till today. What is wrong with this picture? Even though the land area of Israel is about the size of the state of New Jersey and the Arabs control *640* times as much land (see *Comfort, Comfort My People* by M. Basillia Schlink [4]), yet they are the poor *sufferers* at the hands of the imperialistic Israelis. What a coup in the propaganda war! The good news is that this issue will not be settled by propaganda, but by the immutable, faithful God of Abraham, Isaac, and Jacob.

In the end, of course, as with everything, the battle is in a different dimension. God has a will in this matter. There are honest Arabs and Palestinians who are completely sincere about the righteousness of their cause. There are also plenty of Israelis who are only wicked and self-serving atheists. In fact, the most recent polls have for the first time recorded that more than 50 percent of Israelis even *believe* in God. This should be all the evidence we need to see that God's restoration is as He described it in Ezekiel 36:23-24:

Israel at the End of the Twentieth Century

"And I will sanctify My great name, which has been profaned among the nations, which you have profaned in their midst; and the nations shall know that I am the Lord," says the Lord God, "when I am hallowed in you before their eyes. For I will take you from among the nations, gather you out of all countries, and bring you into your own land."

God is still planning on being hallowed in the people of Israel before the watching eyes of the whole world! They have a long way to go, and I confess that I don't know exactly *how* He will do it, but He *will* do it for His *name's* sake. Concurrent with all the political wrangling and posturing for "peace talks," God is steadily going about His business and watching over His Word to bring it to completion.

Look at one more example from Isaiah 27:6: "Those who come He shall cause to take root in Jacob; Israel shall blossom and bud, and fill the face of the world with fruit." Israel is quietly becoming the breadbasket of the Middle East and even Eastern Europe, as seen in this report from the Jerusalem Post: "In the period between Oct. 1 and March 31, Israel exported 100,000 tons of fruits and vegetables and 550 million flowers. Local producers exported 8,500 tons of hothouse tomatoes to Europe and the United States, bringing in a total of $13 million."(5) Israeli oranges are on the shelves of some supermarkets in the United States and have even been seen in Florida supermarkets! Can a nation be born in a day? Israel is alive and well, but will all Jews return to the Holy Land?

GOD IS FAITHFUL!

Chapter 19

The Wilderness on the Way to Promise

A curious phenomena is occurring in conjunction with the great exodus out of the "land of the North." All of these Jewish people are not going directly to Israel. Most of them would prefer going to America or Western Europe. Why do the Jews who escape the tyranny and anti-Semitism of their various persecutors often flee to other countries instead of Israel, even though the national homeland has finally been reestablished as a Jewish sanctuary? In 1990, the U.S. actually had to limit the Jewish quota admitted here to 50,000 per year to prevent overwhelming the U.S. immigration structure. Why don't the Jews just all go pouring into Israel? We would think they would all return to Israel with great joy, but paradoxically, many Jews are fleeing to the West instead of to the Promised Land. Is this thwarting the will of God? The answer is a surprising "no." This occurence was prophesied thousands of years ago by Israel's prophet Ezekiel, as recorded in chapter 20 of the Book of Ezekiel.

Before we look at the answer, though, we need to remind ourselves of the conditions of the dispersion. Moses spoke of what it would be like when Israel was plucked and scattered from their land:

Then the Lord will scatter you among all peoples, from one end of the earth to the other, and there you shall serve other gods, which neither you nor your fathers have known—wood and stone. And among those nations you shall find no rest, nor shall the sole of your foot have a resting place; but there the Lord will give you a trembling heart, failing eyes, and anguish of soul. Your life shall hang in doubt before you; you shall fear day and night, and have no assurance of life. In the morning you shall say, "Oh, that it were evening!" And at evening you shall say, "Oh, that it were morning!" because of the fear which terrifies your heart, and because of the sight which your eyes see (Deuteronomy 28:64-67).

They are also very melancholy, which can be seen in history and in Psalm 137:1-6:

By the rivers of Babylon, there we sat down, yea, we wept when we remembered Zion. We hung our harps upon the willows in the midst of it. For there those who carried us away captive asked of us a song, and those who plundered us requested mirth, saying, "Sing us one of the songs of Zion!" How shall we sing the Lord's song in a foreign land? If I forget you, O Jerusalem, let my right hand forget its skill! If I do not remember you, let my tongue cling to the roof of my mouth—if I do not exalt Jerusalem above my chief joy.

Yet many of the Jews who are released from bondage refuse to return to the land of Israel. Why?

Coming to America

Is God surprised and saying, "Oh no! What am I going to do now? They are missing My plan"? On the contrary, this phenomenon is another amazing literal fulfillment of Bible prophecy. I was discussing this issue with Stephen Peck, my good friend and fellow elder at our church, when he pointed out that the answer was in Ezekiel 20. It gives a remarkable explanation of this paradox, beginning with what has now become the familiar language of the regathering of Israel. Verse 34 helps pinpoint the return, which is distinguished from Egypt or Babylon by the use of the plural forms, "out from the peoples" and "out of the countries." But the next verse, instead of promising their immediate entrance to the land of Israel, specifies this: "And I will bring you into the wilderness of the peoples, and there I will plead My case with you face to face" (Ezek. 20:35). There is a clear statement that they will have to go through a "wilderness of the peoples." Then, to prevent any misunderstanding and for double emphasis, the Lord makes a direct comparison to the Egyptian exodus: " 'Just as I pleaded My case with your fathers in the wilderness of the land of Egypt, so I will plead My case with you,' says the Lord God" (Ezek. 20:36). This Egyptian exodus analogy is again used for the endtimes in reference to Russia and Eastern Europe.

God says He will bring them to a wilderness experience to plead His case with them "face to face" and as in the wilderness of Egypt: " 'Just as I pleaded My case with your fathers in the wilderness of the land of Egypt, so I will plead My case with you,' says the Lord God" (Ezek. 20:36). God is not worried that many Jews are leaving their captivity and coming to America rather than going to Israel. It is part of His eternal plan.

The Rod of God

Psalm 23 is perhaps the most well-known and oft-quoted portion of Scripture in the entire Bible, and it can help us here. The end of verse 4 says, "Your rod and Your staff, they comfort me." Now it is easy to appreciate the shepherd's staff comforting me because it represents the gentle leading to the green pastures and quiet waters of God's care and provision. But I am also comforted by His rod! With the rod, He drives away the enemies and most importantly, corrects me if I head down the wrong path or persist in straying from His presence. So let's apply this thought to understanding the wilderness on the way to promise for the dispersed people of Israel.

We could easily enumerate humanistic reasons for their choice to go the wrong way, such as family ties or the economic pursuit of "the American dream." But the real reason is the one that God gives in Ezekiel 20:37-38:

I will make you pass under the rod, and I will bring you into the bond of the covenant; I will purge the rebels from among you, and those who transgress against Me; I will bring them out of the country where they dwell, but they shall not enter the land of Israel. Then you will know that I am the Lord.

The main function of the wilderness is to purge out the rebels.

There are four specific stages listed here in God's rebel purging process: (a) bring out to the wilderness; (b) plead His case; (c) pass under the rod; and (d) bring into the "bond" of covenant. We can see this process at work as well in our own personal lives and experiences, I am sure. The last stage of the process brings Israel into the bond of covenant. This means they will *return to the Lord as they return to the land.* I am not saying they will accept Messiah Jesus first, but they will return to the knowledge of God. Something will be happening in their hearts. God will examine each one, much as a shepherd looks over every inch of his sheep for any possible injuries, as they come back into the fold for the night. Those who refuse to submit to this process will be purged out of the people of Israel and *will not return to the land*! This is clear in Exodus 20:39 where He says if they will not obey, then "Go, serve every one of you his idols." Those are the words that I pray none of us ever hear from the mouth of God. When God releases someone from His presence, there is no greater judgment. It is the ultimate death sentence. That prospect is more fearsome to me than a hundred sermons about the hellfire and brimstone that awaits the final day of awful reckoning! This process has the effect of producing the knowledge of God in those who submit. "...Then you will know that I am the Lord" (Ezek. 20:38). Praise the Lord!

A Sweet Aroma

The remaining part of this prophecy turns to the work that God will *complete* in them, back in the land of Israel. God speaks of His purpose to purify them in the land. This agrees with Ezekiel 37 about the bones coming together before the life-breath is given. God will *accept* them there as a *sweet aroma.*

> *"For on My holy mountain, on the mountain height of Israel," says the Lord God, "there all the house of Israel, all of them in the land, shall serve Me; there I will*

accept them, and there I will require your offerings and the firstfruits of your sacrifices, together with all your holy things. I will accept you as a sweet aroma when I bring you out from the peoples and gather you out of the countries where you have been scattered; and I will be hallowed in you before the Gentiles" (Ezekiel 20:40-41).

That last phrase agrees with what we previously studied in Ezekiel 36:23. The nations will see that Israel worships God again as the Holy One of Israel!

The prophecy continues with the unmistakable reference again to the land. "Then you shall know that I am the Lord, when I bring you into the land of Israel, into the country for which I raised My hand in an oath to give to your fathers" (Ezek. 20:42). You simply cannot spiritualize this passage and eliminate the literal nature intended by this prophecy. Also once again (as in Ezekiel 36:7), God refers to lifting His hand in an oath about the promise of the "land" and "country" that He gave to Israel's "fathers."

God also includes in this prophecy of Ezekiel 20, their repentance and knowledge of the Lord. But again He states unequivocally that this mercy is "for My name's sake, not according to your wicked ways..." (Ezek. 20:44). God is not worried about what men think of Him. Even Jesus made no reputation for Himself. God is committed to His word *above His name* in Psalm 138:2: "I will worship toward Your holy temple, and praise Your name for Your lovingkindness and Your truth; for You have magnified Your word above all Your name." The principle of Romans 9:15 can also be applied here: "For He says to Moses, 'I will have mercy on whomever I will have mercy, and I will have compassion on whomever I will have compassion.' " He just happens to have revealed in Scripture that He *intends* to have mercy on Israel at the end of time and bring to pass all His great and precious promises to their fathers for His holy name's sake!

In conclusion, there is great excitement (and rightly so) concerning what is happening in the land of Israel today. However, I am also making a strong case for what is happening right here in America and other Western nations. This is where the action is, at least regarding the wondrous purging process that is bringing many to the revelation of God. The Almighty is pleading His case with the Jews and bringing them under the rod of discipline in America (both North and South America). We should not neglect or diminish the significance of God's work *outside* the land.

Moses once said an amazing thing when a couple of men missed the elders' meeting and started prophesying in the camp: "So Joshua the son of Nun, Moses' assistant, one of his choice men, answered and said, 'Moses my lord, forbid them!' Then Moses said to him, 'Are you zealous for my sake? Oh, that all the Lord's people were prophets and that the Lord would put His Spirit upon them!' " (Num. 11:28-29) The same is true today. You may not be a Moses, or even one of those in the elders' gathering. But are you willing to prophesy with the Holy Spirit of God? Many will be called as fishers and even hunters to prophesy the word of the Lord God of Israel among the nations of this second exodus and wilderness experience. They are on the way to Promise. Where do you fit in? Are you ready to submit to the obedience of the Lord?

GOD IS FAITHFUL!

Chapter 20

The Church at the End of the Twentieth Century

Is God finished with the Gentiles? Contrary to the impression given by my emphasis on Israel, I have a heart and vision for the Christian Church which is still overwhelmingly comprised of Gentiles. So for this final chapter, we'll revisit the premise that the Jews will be saved. Then we'll turn to the timing of the turning point of history. Next, we will look at what happens to the nations. Last, we'll see the role of the Church at the end of the twentieth Century.

Opening Blind Eyes

I hope we have put to rest by now the notion that God is through with the Jewish people. But if they are going to be saved, the question is when. Some say never; some say after Jesus comes during the millennium. My view is that it is happening right now, and will continue to happen right up to Jesus' second coming. Some of us are old enough to remember when a Jew would not utter the name of Jesus except as a curse word.

We could not have a conversation at all on the subject. It is now common to debate Jesus vigorously with our Jewish friends in open dialogue. In Israel, there is a noticeable difference every time I visit. During our first tour in 1984, we were warned not to use the name of Jesus when talking to Israelis. On our second trip, we had some delightful ministry with a young sabra (native-born Israeli) who ran a shop in the Jewish quarter of the Old City. We were able to give her a testimony book in Hebrew, and corresponded with her after we were back in the States. During our trip in 1988, we saw an article in the daily *Jerusalem Post* that was discussing the concept of a fourth stream of Judaism. The main three have been Orthodox, Conservative, and Reformed. But that article was about *Messianic* Judaism as the fourth stream! Of course, there is much controversy over the issue, but at least it is an issue. It is being discussed! On our most recent trip in 1990, we were amazed at how open it had become. Most Israelis were willing to discuss the claims of Jesus to be their Messiah.

There are now thousands of Messianic believers in Israel. I spoke in a congregation in January 1990 that, at that time, numbered about 300 committed believers. Eighty-five percent were Israeli Jewish believers, five to seven percent were Israeli Arab believers, and the rest were Gentile believers from other countries. There is also a worldwide Messianic movement with congregations in many nations and language groups, with more than 140 of the groups in the U.S. alone (according to a Spring 1992 listing in *The Messianic Times*, a good newspaper of the movement published in the U.S. and Canada)(1).

Do Jews have the same standing before God as every other people group in the world? The answer is "no." They have a distinct *disadvantage*, or at least they did until recently. God had blinded their eyes to the truth that Jesus is the Messiah, or the way it sounds in Hebrew: Yeshua Ha Meshiach! But God is now in the process of removing the veil and healing their spiritual eyes and ears so they might have as much opportunity to be saved as the Gentiles have had for 1,900 years. Remember that *conversion* from paganism reflects our belief in the One who is the *object* of our worship. *Repentance* of our sins reflects our attitudes with regard to our depraved *life styles*. Whether we are Jew or Gentile, if Jesus becomes the object of our worship, God the Father will save us and forgive our sins.

But if they confess their iniquity and the iniquity of their fathers, with their unfaithfulness in which they were unfaithful to Me, and that they also have walked contrary to Me, and that I also have walked contrary to them and have brought them into the land of their enemies; if their uncircumcised hearts are humbled, and they accept their guilt—then I will remember My covenant with Jacob, and My covenant with Isaac and My covenant with Abraham I will remember; I will remember the land (Leviticus 26:40-42).

That agrees with Ezekiel 37:12-14:

Therefore prophesy and say to them, "Thus says the Lord God: 'Behold, O My people, I will open your graves and cause you to come up from your graves, and bring you into the land of Israel. Then you shall know that I am the Lord, when I have opened your graves, O My people, and brought you up from your graves. I will put My Spirit in you, and you shall live, and I will place you in your own land. Then you shall know that I, the Lord, have spoken it and performed it,' says the Lord."

I will mention one more Scripture to establish that God is the One who blinded them, so He can let them see when it is time. "Just as it is written: 'God has given them a spirit of stupor, eyes that they should not see and ears that they should not hear, to this very day' " (Rom. 11:8). The day Paul spoke of was his day, but in our day the spirit of stupor has been removed! That certainly does not automatically save them, but it allows them to see and decide for themselves. But now let us turn to the timing question.

History Turns

Secular historians will loudly disagree with me, but I see 1967's Six Day War as the greatest turning point of history since the life of Jesus. What is behind such a bold claim? It is my humble opinion that the "times of the Gentiles" has ended! To better understand this concept, let us first find out what it means and why I say it has passed.

Paul makes a bold declaration in Romans 11:25: "For I do not desire, brethren, that you should be ignorant of this mystery, lest you should be wise in your own opinion, that blindness in part has happened to Israel until the fullness of the Gentiles has come in." He said we who are saved (which at first included 99 percent Jews and now is probably exactly the opposite proportion: 99 percent Gentiles), should not be arrogant about the blindness on Israel. He then uses perhaps the most overlooked word in the verse: the word *until*. This is a timing word. It puts the blindness into a context of limited duration! (It also puts a limit on the period of the Gentiles.)

So what is this Gentile time period? Is there anything else about it in the Bible? Of course there is, and it comes from no other than Jesus: "And they will fall by the edge of the sword, and be led away captive into all nations. And Jerusalem will be trampled by Gentiles until the times of the Gentiles are fulfilled" (Lk. 21:42). Among His other titles, we must add one of "prophet" because there are no more precise prophecies anywhere in the Bible. He had been speaking of the fall of Jerusalem, which happened in history approximately 35 years later in 70 A.D. In verse 20 He had clearly spoken of its soon fall and that *they* would see it. Then, after prophesying the scattering, in verse 24, He reveals the incredible detail that Jerusalem is to be dominated by Gentiles from that very time *until* a certain specified time. There's that timing word again! Jerusalem is ruled by Gentiles from 70 A.D. until when? Historically, we now know it to be June 1967. Some scholars tried to date the time of the Gentiles to the Balfour Declaration in 1917. Others dated it with the rebirth of Israel in 1948. Some prefer to say it will not be until the temple is rebuilt. But what did Jesus say? Not at the good will of Britain, or the restoration of the land, or anything about the temple; Jesus said that the key turning point would be when *Jerusalem* came back from Gentile domination.

So we see that Jerusalem becomes the double key to unlocking the prophecies of the endtimes. Paul saw it in Romans 11 and warned us not to be ignorant or arrogant about what it would mean: the key to the duration of Israel's blindness and the grafting in again of Israel. Jesus saw it as the key to the duration of the "times of the Gentiles." It is both. So then does it mean God is finished with the Gentiles? No. He has passed the time when He dealt primarily with proclaiming the gospel to the Gentiles. He is now turning His attention back to the land, to the people and promises of Israel. Does this mean no more Gentiles can be saved? Of course not; the door is still open for all who will call on the name of the Lord Jesus. It is similar to the fact that there were Jews who accepted the Messiah all through the 1,900 years.

There are two big differences since that momentous date in 1967. First, it was the signal for removing the spirit of stupor or of blindness. Second, it was a terrific marker of these end days. Back in Luke 21, Jesus spoke of a number of other signs that would point toward His second coming, including the budding of the fig tree, which I believe refers to the restoration of the land of Israel. He then said, "Assuredly, I say to you, this generation will by no means pass away till all things take place" (Lk. 21:32). He was certainly not speaking of their day. Their generation did pass away, so He had to be speaking of a future generation that would live to see it happen. It is all coming together now, and the key is the restoration of Jerusalem to Jewish rule. It is my personal conviction that the last generation of history is alive today. It was marked by that amazing little Six Day War in 1967.

Derek Prince tells a wonderful story in his book:

I would now like to relate some experiences of a friend that I believe will provide insight into how God views this whole process.

My friend, whom I will call "Pastor W" is an internationally recognized Bible teacher of proven integrity and maturity.

Sometime in the late '50s or early '60s, Pastor W was taking part in a home prayer meeting, when he was granted a vision of a scene in heaven. He saw a great throng of angels with their faces turned toward the earth. They were eagerly following events taking place on earth; and they obviously desired to participate in them. But a golden cord stretched in front of the angels held them back in their place in heaven. Pastor W was left wondering what this vision might mean.

Some years later, in another prayer meeting, he had a similar vision of the angels in heaven with the golden cord holding them back. This time, however, while Pastor W watched, the golden cord was drawn aside. Immediately, with obvious joy and excitement, the whole throng of angels descended to earth. Then the vision ended, and Pastor W was not able to see what the angels proceeded to do on earth.

Pastor W concluded that a sovereign angelic visitation was about to take place; and he began to tell his Christian friends to expect some tremendous work of the Holy Spirit in the area in which he had received the two visions.

Time passed, however, and nothing of special significance happened. Pastor W was disappointed and nonplused, although he could not doubt the authenticity of his two visions.

After a considerable lapse of time, it occurred to him to check back over major world events that had occurred around the time of his second vision—the one in which the angels had been released to participate in the affairs of earth. Perhaps the vision was associated with some development in the world situation that was particularly significant from heaven's viewpoint. He quickly made a discovery that left no doubt as to the meaning of his second vision: *the day he received that vision was the first day of the Six-Day War.*(2)

My wife Doreen and I also have a personal reason to be aware of that time. We were married on June 11, 1967, and have always had an affinity for Israel in our life and ministry. I have a strong desire to proclaim this message of God's faithfulness, as seen through Israel, to the gentile Church. If we miss the timing of God's sovereign acts, we could lose track of "time." It is getting so close to the end, or as the cliché goes: It is later than you think! Regular, almost daily manifestations of God's faithfulness in world events are greatly encouraging our faith.

The Nations Rage

Psalm 2:1-2 asks the question: "Why do the nations rage, and the people plot a vain thing? The kings of the earth set themselves, and the rulers take counsel together, against the Lord and against His Anointed...." You can well imagine that if Heaven really is getting set for the final consummation of the ages, and Israel really is at center stage, then you would expect all hell to be opposed to the events. I believe that is precisely the case and I want to be sure I am on God's side in the battle.

It shall be in that day that I will seek to destroy all the nations that come against Jerusalem. And I will pour on the house of David and on the inhabitants of Jerusalem the Spirit of grace and supplication; then they will look on Me whom they pierced. Yes, they will mourn for Him as one mourns for his only son, and grieve for Him as one grieves for a firstborn (Zechariah 12:9-10).

This was also spoken of by the prophet Micah: "Now also many nations have gathered against you, who say, 'Let her be defiled, and let our eye look upon Zion.' But they do not know the thoughts of the Lord, nor do they understand His counsel;

for He will gather them like sheaves to the threshing floor" (Mic. 4:11).

This gathering of the nations must be the prelude to the last battle of Armageddon in the Jezreel Valley where God gathers the sheaves for burning. God will certainly judge the nations in His own time. There will even be some within these nations who turn to God as He is "hallowed" in His people Israel. "Thus says the Lord of hosts: 'In those days ten men from every language of the nations shall grasp the sleeve of a Jewish man, saying, "Let us go with you, for we have heard that God is with you" ' " (Zech. 8:23).

The Church in Plan A

If there is no Plan B, then where does the Church fit in? It should be clear by now: We are part of *the plan*! There is, and always has been, only one plan of God. The Church does not hand the ball over to Israel and shuffle over to the sidelines for the finale. The true believers of Jesus in the Church and in Israel become one. Paul was quite clear in Romans 11:15-18:

> *For if their being cast away is the reconciling of the world, what will their acceptance be but life from the dead? For if the firstfruit is holy, the lump is also holy; and if the root is holy, so are the branches. And if some of the branches were broken off, and you, being a wild olive tree, were grafted in among them, and with them became a partaker of the root and fatness of the olive tree, do not boast against the branches. But if you do boast, remember that you do not support the root, but the root supports you.*

We are not a new tree or a different tree. We were a different tree, but we (Gentiles) have been grafted into the root of Israel!

Whether we like it or not, there is no denying it. So we are warned not to "boast against the branches." I'm afraid that many Christians are guilty of this charge. Paul continues:

You will say then, "Branches were broken off that I might be grafted in." Well said. Because of unbelief they were broken off, and you stand by faith. Do not be haughty, but fear. For if God did not spare the natural branches, He may not spare you either. Therefore consider the goodness and severity of God: on those who fell, severity; but toward you, goodness, if you continue in His goodness. Otherwise you also will be cut off. And they also, if they do not continue in unbelief, will be grafted in, for God is able to graft them in again (Romans 11:19-23).

I think that says it all.

These modern "replacement theologians" are playing with fire. It is anti-Semitic and anti-God. They are still contending for an interpretation of what happened in the first century and are in danger of missing what God is doing in the twentieth century. They have it backwards. God never replaced Israel (even though He did remove them for 1,900 years), and He warns that He may also remove the Gentile branches if they become too arrogant. I take this very seriously and I want to warn my brethren: Don't get cocky! We sometimes strut around like proud banty roosters in the barnyard. God is not impressed. We better get tuned in to His immutable, unchangeable, undeniable, *eternally faithful* Word.

We are saved by receiving Jesus as our Messiah. We are all unified with one another by coming to God the same way—through Jesus. What does Paul mean in this passage?

> *For you are all sons of God through faith in Christ Jesus. For as many of you as were baptized into Christ have put on Christ. There is neither Jew nor Greek, there is neither slave nor free, there is neither male nor female; for you are all one in Christ Jesus. And if you are Christ's, then you are Abraham's seed, and heirs according to the promise* (Galatians 3:26-29).

There is much confusion about this passsage that can be solved with a simple distinction. Paul is talking about equal access and equal value to God. He is not referring to placement or function. Neither Paul nor I could deny that there are, in fact, still Jews, Greeks, slaves, free, males, and females. These functions still exist in practice. The apostle even gives instructions regarding those functions between husband and wife in Ephesians 5. Therefore, using the principle of interpreting Scripture by Scripture, we are not free to do away with the sexes or cultures. Greeks today still have a distinct culture, but may be committed believers. In the same way, Jews may retain their cultural distinctives while believing in Jesus. Yet, they are both one in God's sight. Thus our unity is clearly in access and value, and we maintain our distinctions and individuality.

Is the Church "true Israel"? Yes, of course it is, to the degree that we are grafted in; but *so is Israel* "true Israel." They are grafted in again as they receive Jesus. The Church and Israel are one tree!

> *And in that day it shall be that living waters shall flow from Jerusalem, half of them toward the eastern sea and half of them toward the western sea; in both summer and winter it shall occur. And the Lord shall be King*

over all the earth. In that day it shall be—"The Lord is one," and His name one (Zechariah 14:8-9).

The beautiful union of all God's people and all of God's purposes seem to leap from the pages of all 66 books of the Bible once you start seeing it.

The word that Isaiah the son of Amoz saw concerning Judah and Jerusalem. Now it shall come to pass in the latter days that the mountain of the Lord's house shall be established on the top of the mountains, and shall be exalted above the hills; and all nations shall flow to it. Many people shall come and say, "Come, and let us go up to the mountain of the Lord, to the house of the God of Jacob; He will teach us His ways, and we shall walk in His paths. For out of Zion shall go forth the law, and the word of the Lord from Jerusalem. He shall judge between the nations, and rebuke many people; they shall beat their swords into plowshares, and their spears into pruning hooks; nation shall not lift up sword against nation, neither shall they learn war anymore (Isaiah 2:1-4).

So what is left for the Church to do? Plenty. Matthew 4:23 tells what Jesus did, and if we are His Body, we will do the same: "And Jesus went about all Galilee, teaching in their synagogues, preaching the gospel of the kingdom, and healing all kinds of sickness and all kinds of disease among the people." We still have a job to do. "And this gospel of the kingdom will be preached in all the world as a witness to all the nations, and then the end will come" (Mt. 24:14). We should pray for the peace of Jerusalem, knowing that the real peace is available only from Jesus, the Prince of Shalom. "And that every tongue should confess that Jesus Christ is Lord, to the glory of God the Father" (Phil. 2:11). If we are blessed with the opportunity, at some point along the way, we might even get to go up to Jerusalem to celebrate the Feast of Tabernacles and fulfill another prophecy or two. What a day! "And it shall come to pass that everyone who is left of all the nations which came against Jerusalem shall go up from year to year to worship the King, the Lord of hosts, and to keep the Feast of Tabernacles" (Zech. 14:16). Praise the name of the Lord forever!

GOD IS FAITHFUL!

Epilogue

A Call to Action

In light of all that we have considered in this book, we should not leave our subject with only a new understanding of the age-old story, but with a definite and specific commitment to do something about it: *Prophesy!* We must declare the prophetic truth of God at every opportunity. Most people view prophecy in its noun form, referring to a study that compares the Bible and history. But I challenge you to consider the verb "to prophesy" as a mandate and calling of God to tell the world, the Jews, and the Church, what God wants said to all of them. We must do more than study it; we must say it! Speak to the dirt, prophesy to the land, prophesy to the bones! We know the answer to whether the bones will live. They will! The bones of the natural house of Israel will live. They will once again have a spiritual relationship with God the same as the Church, for Jesus is alive! The Messiah of Israel and the Messiah of the Church is the same Man, the Son of God. Every knee will bow under His Lordship, to God the Father's glory, as it says in Philippians 2:10-11: "that at the name of Jesus every knee should bow, of those in heaven, and of those on earth, and of those under the earth, and that every tongue should confess that Jesus Christ is Lord, to the glory of God the Father."

The timing of it all is clearly revealed in Psalm 102:18: "This will be written for the generation to come, that a people yet to be created may praise the Lord." The original Hebrew of the phrase, "the generation to come" is *Ledor akharon*, and means "the last generation"! We are living in the very last generation. We must tell it—proclaim it—publish it!

Pray for the peace of Jerusalem "May they prosper who love you" (Ps. 122:6b). "I have set watchmen on your walls, O Jerusalem; they shall never hold their peace day or night. You who make mention of the Lord, do not keep silent, and give Him no rest till He establishes and till He makes Jerusalem a praise in the earth" (Is. 62:6-7).

I cannot think of a better way to end this book than to repeat the plea of Moses that all would prophesy! When Moses had called all the 70 elders together, two of them didn't make it to the meeting, but the anointing was so strong that those two started to prophesy right in the midst of the people. When some, including Joshua, asked Moses to forbid them, his response was: "Are you zealous for my sake? Oh, that all the Lord's people were prophets and that the Lord would put His Spirit upon them!" (Num 11:29). Tell it! Proclaim it! Publish it!

If you want to know what God would have you do, respond to the word He gave when Isaiah said, "What shall I cry?"

The voice said, "Cry out!" And he said, "What shall I cry?" "All flesh is grass, and all its loveliness is like the

Epilogue: A Call to Action

flower of the field. The grass withers, the flower fades, because the breath of the Lord blows upon it; surely the people are grass. The grass withers, the flower fades, but the word of our God stands forever." O Zion, you who bring good tidings, get up into the high mountain; O Jerusalem, you who bring good tidings, lift up your voice with strength, Lift it up, be not afraid; say to the cities of Judah, "Behold your God!" (Isaiah 40:6-9).

GOD IS FAITHFUL!

References

Chapter 4

1. Earl Paulk, *To Whom Is God Betrothed?* (Atlanta, Georgia: Dimension Publishers, 1985).

2. Steve Lightle, *Exodus II* (Kingwood, Texas: Hunter Books, 1983).

Chapter 5

1. James Strong, *Strong's Concordance* Nashville, Tennessee: Thomas Nelson Publishers, Greek lexicon #2907 and #4561.

2. Kevin J. Conner and Ken Malmin, *Interpreting the Scriptures* (Portland, Oregon: Bible Temple Publications, 1983).

3. Bernard Ramm, *Protestant Biblical Interpretation* (Boston, Massachusetts: W.A. Wilde Company, 1956).

4. Rousas John Rushdoony, *The Institutes of Biblical Law* (Phillipsburg, New Jersey: The Presbyterian and Reformed Publishing Company, 1973).

Chapter 7

1. *Cassell's German Dictionary* (New York: Macmillan Publishing Company, 1978), pp. 182, 293. (Note: I have not been able to document the reports I have heard that *Khrushchev* means "clay" in Ukrainian.)

Chapter 8

1. Ron Blue, *Master Your Money* (Nashville: Thomas Nelson Publishers, 1986), p. 15.

Chapter 11

1. Derek Prince, *The Last Word on the Middle East* (Derek Prince Ministries International, P.O. Box 300, Ft. Lauderdale, Florida 33302-0300, 1982), pp. 101-102.

2. Ibid., p. 103. Derek Prince's Scripture references are from the New International Version, © 1978 by New York International Bible Society; published by The Zondervan Corporation, Grand Rapids, Michigan, 49506.

Chapter 13

1. Daniel Pipes, *National Review* 11-19-90, p. 28.

2. David Dolan, *Holy War for the Promised Land* (Nashville, Tennessee: Thomas Nelson Publishers, 1991), pp. 38-39.

3. Ibid., p. 39.

4. Rousas John Rushdoony, *The Institutes of Biblical Law* (Phillipsburg, New Jersey: The Presbyterian and Reformed Publishing Company, 1973), pp. 32-33.

5. Francis Schaeffer, *The Church Before The Watching World*, (Wheaton, Illinois: Crossway Books, 1985), pp. 145-146.

6. Professor Peter A. Michas, *What Is Islam?* (Poway, California: The Christian Mid-East Conference, 1991).

References

7. Derek Prince, *The Last Word On The Middle East* (Derek Prince Ministries International, P.O. Box 300, Ft. Lauderdale, Florida 33302-0300, 1982), pp. 68-69.

8. David Dolan, *Holy War for the Promised Land* (Nashville, Tennessee: Thomas Nelson Publishers, 1991), pp. 46,42-43,57.

9. Dr. Gayle Kesselman, *About Islam* (Kesselman Foundation, P.O. Box 809, Boynton Beach, Florida).

10. David Dolan, *Holy War for the Promised Land* (Nashville, Tennessee: Thomas Nelson Publishers, 1991), p. 213.

11. Ibid., p. 217.

12. Daniel Pipes, *National Review*, 11-19-90, p. 30.

13. Ibid.

14. David Dolan, *Holy War for the Promised Land* (Nashville, Tennessee: Thomas Nelson Publishers, 1991), pp. 172-173.

15. Ibid., p. 209.

Chapter 14

1. David Dolan, *Holy War for the Promised Land* (Nashville, Tennessee: Thomas Nelson Publishers, 1991), p. 30.

2. *The Zion Quarterly* 3rd Quarter, 1992 (Jerusalem: Christian Friends of Israel), p. 1.

3. Thomas L. Friedman, *From Beirut to Jerusalem* (New York: Farrar Straus Giroux, 1989), p. 77.

Chapter 16

1. David Dolan, *Holy War for the Promised Land* (Nashville, Tennessee: Thomas Nelson Publishers, 1991), pp. 26-27.

2. Ibid., pp. 30-31.

3. Earl Paulk, *To Whom Is God Betrothed?* (Atlanta, Georgia: Dimension Publishers, 1985)

4. Ibid., p. 15.

5. Keith Parker's pamphlet "Is the Church the New Israel: A Biblical Analysis of the Teachings of Replacement Theology" can be obtained from the following address: Prayer for Israel, P.O. Box 1, Golant, Cornwall, United Kingdom.

6. Steve Lightle, *Exodus II*, (Kingswood, Texas: Hunter Books, 1983).

Chapter 17

1. Derek Prince, *The Last Word on the Middle East* (Derek Prince Ministries International, P.O. Box 300, Ft. Lauderdale, Florida 33302-0300, 1982), pp. 116-117.

2. Meridel Rawlings, *Fishers and Hunters* (Ontario: World Vistas Inc., 1982), pp. 3-4.

Chapter 18

1. Derek Prince, *The Last Word on the Middle East* (Derek Prince Ministries International, P.O. Box 300, Ft. Lauderdale, Florida 33302-0300, 1982), p. 47.

2. Robert St. John, *Tongue of the Prophets* (North Hollywood, California: Wilshire Book Company, 1952).

3. *Zion Quarterly*, 3rd Quarter, 1992 (Jerusalem: Christian Friends of Israel), p. 1.

4. M. Basilica Schlink, *Comfort, Comfort My People* (Darmstadt-Eberstadt, West Germany: Evangelical Sisterhood of Mary, 1989), pp. 13-17.

5. "Farm Exports Blossom," *Jerusalem Post*, 4-21-90.

References

Chapter 20
1. *The Messianic Times*, (P.O. Box 1191, Lewiston, New York 14092).
2. Derek Prince, *The Last Word on the Middle East* (Derek Prince Ministries International, P.O. Box 300, Ft. Lauderdale, Florida 33302-0300, 1982), p. 96.

Les Lawrence is available for speaking engagements and seminars. He also leads occasional tours to Israel. If you are interested in scheduling him to speak to your congregation or organization, please contact him at the following address. You may also order this book directly from him.

Les Lawrence
Maranatha Chapel
1148 E. Turner St.
Clearwater, FL 34616
(813) 461-1148